Smart Women, Inspired Lives

How to Be Happy & Confident

Dr. Lisa Kaplin

Contents

Dedication

This book is dedicated to all of the women in my life who have inspired me, motivated me, loved and accepted me. When I look around, I see an embarrassment of riches to call them friends, colleagues, family, and clients. Yet my biggest inspiration and source of motivation is my incredible daughter, Michelle. Watching her grow into the amazing young woman she is today has been the greatest gift of all.

Introduction

L ike many women I know, I've spent most of my life trying to make other people happy. It's what lots of us were raised to do; be good girls, don't start trouble, and please others first. I was good at it, really good. Yet I was miserable. My confidence was essentially non-existent and I found very little joy in a life that had all the necessary components needed to find happiness.

There were many little red flags along the way, but the biggest came in the form of my children commenting on how little I laughed and how unhappy I often seemed to be. I was modeling martyr behavior and a life only partially lived. It was time to change and thus I started on my journey to find both confidence and happiness regardless of what was going on around me.

I read everything I could get my hands on, I asked others, and then I started to gather the tools that led to the confident and joyful life that I now live. This isn't some rose-colored-glasses-ignore-the-bad-stuff story. It's the culmination of many life lessons learned through education and experience that brought me to this point. It's also what led me to work with clients who have been struggling with the very same issues and ultimately to write this book.

Working with women has been the fulfillment of a life long dream and what I was meant to do. Women seek my services for many reasons, but ultimately they struggle with a lack of happiness and very limited confidence. When they find each of these, anything is possible. Finding my own joy and confidence was fabulous; helping others to do the same is even better.

CHAPTER 1

Start Speaking Up NOW

It's only scary until you start doing it ...
then life gets awesome!

You know you want to be happy and confident. The two go hand in hand. The more confident you are, the happier you feel. The happier you are, the more confidence you exude. Both are skills you can acquire and your "training" starts now.

It's time to quit feeling sorry for ourselves, ladies, for not getting our needs met, for not being heard, and for not going to our favorite restaurant. There is a simple solution. We need to SPEAK UP for what we want.

This is the year you begin to ask for what you want—clearly, concisely, kindly, yet unapologetically. It's no secret that it's damaging to your psyche, your confidence, and your relationships to not speak up, yet, here we are still talking about it. It's time to figure out what we need to do differently and then do it. It's time to reap the rewards of a life that we choose to live, and not one that we just react to.

So what are you missing? Why do you keep promising yourself to speak up in relationships, at work, in meetings, and at social occasions, and yet you find yourself holding back at exactly the wrong moment?

Don't be too hard on yourself. You've grooved a deep pattern both in your behaviors and in your brain that's challenging to overcome without the right amount of information and energy. I'm here to help, sister.

I've been in your shoes; they were tight, they hurt, and they kept me from leading a really fabulous life. But that was then and this is now. I learned to speak up and my life has definitely changed for the better.

Here are the steps I took to change it:

1. Figure out exactly what you want. Not what others want for you.

A few years ago, if you had asked me what I wanted out of life, I would have given you an answer that reflected what mattered to my loved ones, with hardly a glimmer of what mattered to me. Whose fault was this? Mine.

I put others first and lost sight of myself. By doing so, I become resentful, bitter, and just the slightest bit bitchy; yet, I still wasn't speaking up for myself and was just whining.

So, now it's your turn. What do you want out of your life? What makes you happy? What's your favorite color, your favorite restaurant, your favorite TV show? What activities make you joyful and which ones leave you bored? What do you want from a partner? Friends? Work?

It is well past the time for you to figure yourself out. Take the time NOW to answer these questions. Write down what you want. (If you have trouble with this exercise, reach out. I am here to guide you.)

2. Change your mindset about speaking up.

Every time I was about to speak up, something in my brain would trigger and silence me. It sounded like this: *Be quiet. You are going to embarrass yourself or make this person angry and upset. Be a good girl and be quiet.*

This mindset was tough to break. Many of my clients have similar scenarios running through their heads that keep them from speaking up.

But we can change this mindset. I started by thinking, *I matter. My voice matters.* I repeated it again and again until I believed it. Give yourself some time but start with a mantra that works for you. A fearful mindset led to insecure feelings and thus, to rather useless behaviors. Is that how you want to continue to live? I didn't think so.

I changed my mindset and you can too. Start with your thought process, figure out how it's holding you back, and then change it until you believe it.

3. Start saying what you want (without apology).

This can be tough at first. You aren't used to saying what you really want, but neither was I. I started with, "I'd like you to put your own dishes away," and then, "I'm the right person for this job so I want you to hire me," and then "It's not okay to deny women these rights and that's why I'm voting for *so and so*."

Yep, I started very tentatively to speak up. Don't be surprised when the people in your life push back as you start to find your voice. They aren't used to it and they are likely to ignore or disagree with you. Don't wilt back into your corner. This is when you need to summon some big strength, leave your victim thoughts behind, stand up and say it again.

You can do it. Practice, practice, practice. Don't say it louder, simply say it nicely and firmly. Say it!

4. Look to other women for inspiration.

The less I spoke up, the worst I felt about myself. My confidence plummeted, my self-esteem was on hiatus, and I didn't like who I was.

I looked at my incredible teenage daughter and my heart broke because this was not what I wanted to model for her. She deserved a mother who showed her how to do hard things.

Seeing me become strong, powerful, and speaking up for others and myself has helped her to do the same. There has been little else in my life that has brought me as much joy as watching her develop her own voice.

I watched other women who I greatly admired and imitated their assertiveness and well thought-out opinions. I've pushed my clients to do the same. When women speak up, they promote others to do the same. Change yourself and you change the world.

Most of us spend useless energy on resolutions that don't change much in our lives, but learning how to speak up will change every aspect of your life. Happy and confident starts here, now.

Just like Sara Bareilles sings, I too honestly want to see you be brave. The more you speak up, the easier it gets. The more you ask for what you want, the more you get it. That is the key to a happy and confident life.

CHAPTER 2

Rise and shine!

*The easiest way to a happier day is
to stop the morning madness.*

Part of living an inspired life is taking the reins of your own happiness. That starts first thing every morning. So many of my clients tell me that their day begins with dread, anxiety, and overwhelm.

Do you start your day feeling as if you have a thousand-pound weight on your chest? Do you have so many "to do's" running through your head that you have knots in your stomach before you've even had your morning coffee? Do you lie in bed thinking, "I can't handle this day" before the day even begins?

I get it. I used to start my day in the same way practically wishing the day was over before it even began. I'd lie in bed thinking of all that I had to do that day, of how most of it seemed overwhelming, and some of it downright unpleasant.

There weren't enough hours to get it all done, and how much of it did I really want to do?

Yet had you asked me about my life, I would have told you that I have a wonderful family, a job that I love, and many events that I look forward to. That would be the truth. So why the miserable beginning to each day?

It seems that many of us are programmed to start the day looking for the struggle versus the excitement. Unless you live on a beach with a wait staff, you probably have tasks to do during each day that you don't particularly enjoy or a to do list that feels overwhelming. So instead of focusing our first waking moments on the people and events that we really look forward to, we end up focusing on the activities that make us nervous or that we dislike. Not a good way to begin every day.

So what's the answer? Should we avoid all negative tasks and people so that we can just wake up without a care in the world? As nice as that sounds, it probably isn't very realistic. The only way to change our morning programming is to change the channel in our brain to learn to look forward to and enjoy most aspects of each day.

You change your programming the way you change a muscle; you work it by changing what you are focusing on. You need to replace the dreaded to do list with another thought in order to start your day feeling motivated. It can be as simple as repeating numerous times, "I've got this day" or "I can handle this." Or you can say something kind and simple to start your day such as, "All is well" or "Today is a good day."

When we change our thinking, we change the way we feel and thus how we take on the day. If you start each day by saying, "I can't handle this," I can guarantee that you won't handle it.

It sounds simplistic yet if you observe happy, motivated people, you won't find that they have any fewer obstacles in their lives than you do. Instead you will find that they face those obstacles with a different mindset. It isn't a case of rose colored glasses or false sounding affirmation type of behavior, but rather a true focus on the things that they look forward to or that bring them joy within their day.

What is that for you? Take a few moments now to concentrate on how you would prefer to start your day. Maybe you can look forward to your cup of coffee, or getting your kids on the bus, or those fifteen minutes that you carve out for yourself midday. Be mindful when you wake up to not focus on what you dread, as that only brings more attention to how much you dislike it.

Here's a new way of looking at it. Think of your morning routine as a vaccine for the rest of your day. Give yourself a shot of gratitude and optimism. Don't allow small things to throw you off of that happiness. Instead ask yourself: will I let this situation ruin my whole day or just this minute?

Our days are limited so why spend them in dread and misery? Shake off the bad stuff, look for the good, and make your morning madness into madly fun instead of madly miserable.

Like any habit, it takes a few days to get in the groove, but you can stop dreading your day by making these minor adjustments in the morning. By paying attention to where your thoughts go and bringing them back to a positive focus, you will feel much happier and more confident. It is empowering to know that you really can rise and shine.

CHAPTER 3

A Sweet Good Night

*A positive start and end to each day
can make it easier in the middle.*

In much the same way as we begin our day on a positive note, we need to pay attention to how we wind down at the end of the day. Your behavior in the morning and at night are like bookends and you want to support yourself in the best way possible.

For years, I watched the ten o'clock news. Afterwards, I would get into bed quite sure that the world was filled with terrible people. I saw nasty people everywhere. There were mean people driving on the highway, grumpy people on the train, and rude people all over my life. I saw gossipy people in my community, demanding people at work, and even my own family seemed rather difficult. It was all so discouraging and hopeless.

Then one day, I decided to stop watching the news. I went to bed earlier, read a good book, and woke up genuinely happier. At the same time, I stopped taking every behavior of others as a direct confrontation with me. Most people who are crabby and miserable are that way because of themselves, not because of others. Why did I need to take on their unhappiness?

My happiness is up to me. I started to look for positive, happy, and kind people to be friends with, and I distanced myself from those who were not very enjoyable to be around.

Suddenly, there seemed to be a lot of really good people in the world.

There were drivers who waived people ahead in a traffic jam. I witnessed helpful people on the train who made room for others or helped carry heavy bags. I started to observe random acts of kindness all around me by so many people. Where had all of these people been hiding? Had the world suddenly changed right before my eyes?

Apparently not. It turns out that I had changed. In doing so, I had changed my focus. It's like walking into a department store to look for a pair of black pants. All you see are a variety of black pants and you miss out on the colorful dresses, the warm coats, and the soft scarves.

When your mind is made up on one idea, it scans for evidence of just that. So when I thought there were only bad people in the world, all I saw were bad people. When I shifted my focus, my vision changed and thus the world that I lived in changed as well.

I didn't put on blinders or the oft-referred-to rose colored glasses in order to pretend that the bad was good—it isn't.

Instead, I actively looked for the good and that's where all the good people were. What are you actively looking for?

One simple bedtime habit made a huge impact on my happiness level. Letting go of tuning into the late news was easy and extremely beneficial. I am not burying my head in the sand. I don't ignore the news. I follow the news, but I follow it in smaller doses and at my own discretion. I choose when to acknowledge the bad and how to care for those I love because of it. Yet I also, very carefully, choose the good. I choose the good news, the good stories, and most especially the good people.

It turns out the world is filled with colorful, joyful, kind, and compassionate people. They are funny and silly and helpful and in every way as interesting and fabulous as you would want them to be. There are people who do good things without waiting for recognition and there are people who are braver and more daring than I ever thought possible. They are here. The good people are right here waiting to be found.

They are in your world too. Start to look for them. Seek and you will find. Living an inspired life means you allow yourself to be inspired. That can be as simple as shutting off the news and implementing a new bedtime habit. Think back on one interaction that uplifted you. This small exercise makes a world of difference. See how it changes your world and provides a sweeter good night.

CHAPTER 4

Gratitude Made Simple

Find your place on the gratitude bandwagon.

Thanksgiving in America is a time in which we give thanks for all of the blessings and gifts in our lives. I love Thanksgiving, but more for the food than the forced gratitude day. Call me a Thanksgiving Scrooge, but sometimes the push for gratitude feels oppressive and I feel guilty for not having that deep enlightened gratitude awareness. I am grateful for many things in my life, yet the trendy push for gratitude (social media, anyone?) can be overwhelming.

Face it, not all of us are Zen enough to be grateful for some of the crap that comes our way. "Be grateful for your cancer diagnosis!" "Be grateful for all the funerals you attended this year." "Be grateful for losing your job." Well, you get the idea. I'm not sure that we always need to be "grateful." It's a lot of pressure. On the other hand, I have seen how much my own mood and mindset can shift when I look and find things to be grateful for.

My gratitude practice might look a tad bit less intense than other versions, but it really works for me. Every day I write down three things that I'm grateful for, but they can't be the same three things every day. And although I am grateful daily for my three children, my husband, and my dog (not always in that order), I look for three unique things to be grateful for each day. Coffee hits my list regularly, but I won't allow myself to put it on my list every day. That's just too easy. Chocolate has hit the list a few key times as well.

Some examples of my gratitude list:

- A sunny day
- A working car
- Work
- Clients
- A cat nap (taken with above mentioned dog)
- Not yelling at anyone
- Catching an earlier train
- Not honking my horn for a whole day
- Short meetings
- My favorite song on the radio
- An empty house (except for me and above mentioned dog)
- A hot shower
- Carry out

- Pizza delivery
- A weekend with nothing scheduled
- My laptop
- A great book and time to read it
- My hammock and time to lay in it
- Slow cookers
- When my kids show signs of being really good people
- A walk with my dog
- A great book on tape (I know, they aren't really on tape anymore)
- A new episode of The Big Bang Theory

Here's the bottom line—Not all of us are grateful all the time and for all things. That seems pretty normal to me. So cut yourself some slack if you are not always basking in gratitude. Yet the feeling and mindset of gratitude is a powerful one that can bring us great joy and contentment.

So what are some simple, even silly things that you can be grateful for? When you think of them, notice the slight shift in your mood or your emotional energy level. With time, you will be reminded of what is so wonderful about our world. And let me say it right now, thank you dear reader, I am truly grateful for you.

CHAPTER 5

Happiness Lessons From My Dog

Happiness really is a warm puppy.

You may have noticed that I am grateful for my dog. Ginger is my seventy-five pound, energy-filled Goldendoodle who joined our family almost eight years ago. I claimed that we got her for my children, but in actuality it was because I was lonely that year when my youngest child went off to school. My house was quiet and I was lost and unhappy. The demands of motherhood were decreasing and I'd put everyone and everything before my career, my own fulfillment, and me. I was moody, lonely, and not sure how to change the course of my own life and happiness.

I know I'm not alone because I meet so many women who feel the same way. Who knew that my sweet puppy would pull me out of this unhappiness and that observing her behavior would push me to change my own? Through my fog of feeling sorry for myself and not sure where to turn, I was able to observe some profound doggy behaviors that I decided to mirror. Maybe these will help you too.

1) Don't take things so personally.

When Ginger first joined our family, we made quite a few mistakes with her. My husband accidentally stepped on her tail. I left her in her crate for longer than I should have for the first few nights she was with us. And one time I accidentally left her in a dark garage for a couple of hours. After each of these incidents, she licked our faces and moved on. Just like that, we were forgiven and invited to rub her belly. What a concept!

For much of my life, I would take things that others said so personally. I would harbor resentment and stay in my pissed off misery for days, weeks or months. I'm not sure who I thought I was hurting, but the answer is clearly myself. Revenge came in the form of my own unhappiness over some imagined and/ or real offenses by others. Ginger doesn't love everyone and she doesn't bother with those that she isn't interested in; the rest of the world has automatic forgiveness in her book. I've followed suit.

2) Ask for what you want and feel free to be a bit bossy about it.

We know what Ginger wants because she lets us know. If she wants to go out, she stands at the door, and if necessary, she barks. If she wants to cuddle on the couch, she comes over and stares at us until we make room for her. A treat? She sticks her nose in the pantry until someone sees her and responds to her request. She doesn't get mad if we say no, but she's never afraid to ask.

Frequently, I have been hesitant to ask for what I wanted. I didn't want to be a burden or high maintenance. I wanted to be liked and loved, but not ask for those things. It turns out that most of us can't read minds and simple requests usually lead to lovely responses. When I don't ask for what I want, I'm resentful and miserable. When I do ask, I know exactly where I stand with others.

3) Never give up on your dream.

Ginger's dream appears to be to catch and play with squirrels. She starts each day by chasing them through our yard until they scamper up our trees. Ginger sits at the bottom of the tree with her tail wagging waiting for further interactions. She's never caught a squirrel and they don't seem too interested in play dates with her, yet she never gives up on that dream. Ginger seems to actually have fun day in and day out in her pursuit of squirrels. I now give her words of encouragement before I let her out each morning, "You go girl! Catch that squirrel! Today is your day!" Who knows? Maybe some day they will invite her over for a quick game of tag or catch.

Somewhere between my melancholy misery and my motivational puppy, I adopted the belief in myself that I never give up. My kids might tell you that they don't find that to be my finest quality, but not giving up has carried me far. I started my own business, reinvigorated my marriage, nagged my children (that's the part they don't love), and improved my health, all under the umbrella of not giving up on the dream of my own joyful life. Tenacity, both in squirrel catching and in life, turns out to be a rather fabulous characteristic.

There are days that I look at my sweet dog getting older, slowing down, and needing a few more naps. The powerful lessons that she has taught me remain solid, despite her aging years. She's got a few other qualities that I've decided not to emulate, sniffing butts, and questionable food choices, but who knows? Those might come in handy one day as well.

CHAPTER 6

Don't Dread the Good Stuff

*Do you "get it done and move on"
or do you enjoy your days?*

Recently, I was preparing for a truly busy week. My husband and daughter both had birthdays to celebrate. We were having a going away party for my oldest son who was leaving for a job overseas. It was parent orientation at the high school. A dear friend was having a 50th birthday party. And I was giving a 3-day program on women's assertiveness, with the other two days of my week filled with client sessions. As I was thinking ahead to the week, I heard myself say, "Things will be better when this week is over."

Things will be better? Seriously? What could be better than a week of celebrations and work that makes me deliriously happy? What was wrong with me to be looking forward to such a fabulous week being over? I realized that although these were all events that I love, I was nervous about the intensity and the busyness of the week. I was actually dreading the good stuff.

Had I stayed in that mindset, I would have tolerated a fabulous week. I would have checked off each event and taken a deep breath to get through the rest of it. It would have been no different than checking doctor's appointments off my list. Get it done, move on. There was no conscious awareness on my part that I wasn't present for the good stuff, but rather pushing through in order to get to the next week.

After I made this awareness, I made a huge mindset shift to, "This is going to be a FABULOUS week! I'm going to be present and enjoy every last minute of it. If I'm a bit tired, oh well. It will have been worth it." And that's exactly what I did. I enjoyed every wonderful moment. I celebrated the birthdays. I hosted friends for the going away party for my son. And I dove into my assertiveness talk with outrageous energy and motivation.

My clients got the absolute best of me because I was fully present, excited to see them, and certainly not clicking off the time until our meetings ended. I gave that week and the people in it a full YES and ended the week with energy and gratitude. Now I watch myself carefully for any thoughts of, "Let's just get this week over with." Those thoughts didn't allow me to enjoy the good stuff. Instead, they pushed me to dread the time that is the best of my life.

I'm aware now and change my thoughts from, "This will be a tough/busy week" to "This is going to be a wonderful week filled with all of the things that I love to do and people that I love to spend time with." Life is too short to dread the good stuff and I'm not going to let myself do that anymore. Tough or sad days will still happen, but I'll deal with them when I get there. In the meantime, I can't wait for the good stuff!

Notice how you respond when you look at your calendar for the week. Do you dread or embrace? Give yourself the gift of a mindset shift. Say it with me: This is going to be a wonderful week! Look at all the things I get to do! (If you have trouble with this, reach out to me. This is exactly the kind of thing I help my clients with.)

Make a promise to yourself that life is too short to dread it and that you will be present and enjoy!

CHAPTER 7

What's Done is Done

*Let go of beating yourself up and
rehashing the past.*

I gave one of my clients the assignment of repeating again and again, "What's done is done." Based on her scowling face, I'm pretty sure she didn't like that assignment. Like many of my clients, she seemed to relish the opportunity to beat up on herself over things that she'd done in the past. Why is it that we are so willing to hang on to so-called mistakes from our past and use them to make ourselves miserable in the present?

Do we get some kind of reward for getting down on ourselves and rehashing the past? And how does it serve us to keep reminding ourselves about our rotten mistakes from the past? Can we change the past if we make ourselves miserable enough? Trust me, we can't.

The past is done and we need to take what we can from it and then move the hell on. Anything else is simply torture.

If you find yourself obsessing about some real or perceived mistake from your past, start by asking yourself if you can change what's done. Then ask yourself if you can learn something from it. If the answer is yes, decide what you want to learn and what you want to change for the future. Finally, ask yourself how holding on to this issue from the past is serving you. Is it keeping you from moving forward in some way? Is it allowing you to spend time feeling sorry for yourself? Is that what you want?

Here's a wild idea. What if there are no mistakes? What if we need to be exactly where we are right now and we got here from things that happened in the past? What if there is something to learn from the past or something about it that led to positive change in our lives? Rarely have I looked back on past "mistakes" and not realized how they have led me to big changes and ultimately a better situation.

Maybe I've snapped at one of my children, saw the hurt in their eyes, and realized that I need to change how I talk to them. I apologize sincerely and quickly pledge new behavior, and then practice putting that behavior into action. That "mistake" led to insight and a change in behavior that makes my children and me feel better. If I sat and mulled over what I'd done, nothing would have been gained from my poor behavior.

We all make mistakes and do things that we regret. Welcome to being human! Find a way to understand why you did what you did, how you can do it differently next time, and what you will need to change in order to stop that behavior. Obsessing over it won't help you, those you love, or your ability to change for the future.

It's time to say, "What's done is done" and move on!

CHAPTER 8

Finding Comfort in Discomfort

*The only way we ever truly grow is
when we step out of comfort.*

A topic that comes up again and again for me, my clients, and my friends is the feeling of being uncomfortable when we try new things, change something in our lives, or do something scary. It's uncomfortable to suddenly be assertive and ask for what we want. It's uncomfortable to set limits for ourselves when we've never done it before. It's scary to make a big life change or to face a challenge that seems overwhelming.

When we feel like that, it's completely normal to want to run back to our old ways that feel safe and comfortable. It's hard to change and it's really hard to feel uncomfortable and not do something about that feeling. Yet ultimately, the only way we learn, grow, and change is to get really comfortable in discomfort. We need to push ourselves to stay in that discomfort until we either learn what we are supposed to or we become comfortable with the change.

Most of us get stuck in bad habits or old patterns because they become easy and comfortable for us. We tolerate a bad relationship, or a dead end job, or misbehaving children until we wake up one day and say, "How did I get to this miserable place?" And the truth is that it often seems easier to stay in that place then to push ourselves into discomfort in order to change.

So how do we get comfortable in discomfort? We talk to ourselves. Yep, we remind ourselves that change is uncomfortable and hard. We tell ourselves that if we can hang on, we will feel better soon and the discomfort will have been so worth it. We think of hard things that we've conquered in the past and we remind ourselves that this too shall pass. We keep the end in sight and we reach out for help if we need it.

What have you done in your life that led you to finding comfort in the discomfort? What did it lead to? How did you grow from it? What are you holding yourself back from because you are avoiding that discomfort? What's it going to take for you to dive in and get comfortable with the discomfort?

Were you waiting for a sign? You just got it! Don't think discomfort is bad or wrong. It is exactly what you need to grow! You will come through it wiser and happier and more confident. I promise.

CHAPTER 9

Selfless or Selfish: Are these our only two choices?

Life does not work best at extremes, find your spot on the spectrum.

Here's what my clients tell me, "I need to be completely selfless, that's just who I am. Otherwise I'm being selfish and I'm not happy that way." They tell me this as if women have only two choices in life, to give up everything for others or to only care about themselves. Either way, I've found that my clients are miserable at both ends of this spectrum. And here's the thing, it is a spectrum!

Because it is a spectrum, that means that there are thousands of options between both ends of selfless and selfish. Why do we have so much trouble finding those middle spots?

Maybe we were raised to be "good girls" and we took that to mean that everyone else comes before us. Or maybe we are afraid we will lose people we love if we don't give completely of ourselves? There are myriad reasons that may have gotten us to this place, but none of them are worthy of losing our well-being and joy.

If giving of yourself at all costs brings you contentment and happiness, then do your thing. Yet I've never seen a woman look anything but ragged and exhausted after taking care of others and giving nothing to herself.

Since when did finding time and space for ourselves come to mean that we are selfish?

I'm always amazed when mothers tell me that they feel too guilty when they have a girl's night out or a well-deserved afternoon on their own. Does motherhood mean instant martyrdom? I didn't get that memo and I don't want it. Neither selflessness nor selfishness will be good for our own happiness and productivity or for those around us. If you want to be productive at work, learn how to take care of yourself. If you want to be a good mom, you'd better put your own well-being into the mix.

So how do we get off the selfish/selfless misery train? First, we have to recognize that we are on it. We have to notice the things we are saying to ourselves that are keeping us stuck. Things like, "I have to put everyone else first or things will fall apart." Or, "Poor me, I deserve time for myself and I'm going to take it right now regardless of what's going on at work." One end of that is a true victim mentality and the other end is an angry aggressive mindset—neither one is going to make you happy or content!

Check your thoughts every time you get on the misery train and then do the work you need to do to change how you are thinking about the situation. Selfless and selfish thoughts are normal, but they aren't a bit helpful. Stop for five minutes when you get caught in either of those mindsets and ask yourself a few questions; "What's the best use of my time right now?" "Will I be helping myself and others with my decision or will I just be hurting myself while only helping others? "Am I feeling sorry for myself right now? If so, why?" "Am I angry right now? If so, why?"

By slowly and carefully answering these questions of yourself or of someone who wants to help you, you will start to realize your motivation for your actions. Once you do that, you have the power to change both your mindset and your actions, which will ultimately be better for you and for those around you.

It is not either/or; you can give to others and take care of yourself and EVERYONE benefits. That is the happy train you will want to ride on.

CHAPTER 10

Changing Our Voice

When I finally learned to change my voice,
I was finally able to change myself.

One of my clients was going through a very difficult time. She was ready to just succumb to the unhappiness she was feeling. Understandably, she felt angry, out of control, and pissed off at me and the world. Yet she sent me an email that had this line, *"I realized that I do need to find some happiness in this crazy mess that keeps getting crazier. It is my voice that needs to change. I can't give up on changing what I tell myself even though this thought process has been imbedded in my brain for decades. The negativity is holding me back from moving forward . . ."*

Her email brought tears to my eyes because I know how rotten her situation is, yet she was able to find the courage to dig even deeper. My client realized that she couldn't change the chaos around her, but she could change what she said to herself about it. It's not going to be easy, yet her desire to do so is what will lead her to happiness and calm.

I spent years telling myself a really nasty, negative story. The only person I hurt with that story was myself. It didn't change anyone around me. It didn't improve my relationships. And it certainly didn't make me happy. When I finally learned to change my voice, I was finally able to change myself. That voice still periodically shows up, but I catch it and change it faster than ever before in my life.

When my clients get to the moment in which they realize that changing their voice will change their lives, I know that they are going to be just fabulous. Crappy things happen in our lives and yucky people show up, but how we respond to those people and situations is completely up to us. Changing our voice is hard work, but changing it will bring us peace and joy.

Changing your voice is about what you say internally and externally. I recall when I was on my way home from a life-changing trip to Israel. I was there with 200 other women from all over the country. On the first day of our trip, our fearless leader handed each of us a wristband. She told us that we must switch the band from wrist to wrist every time we complained or gossiped. I was sure that I wouldn't have to change that band even once because I was so grateful and happy to be on this trip.

Almost immediately, I found it necessary to switch the band. I was annoyed at one of our group mates for what I considered to be bragging. A few minutes later, I was aggravated with the hot weather despite the fact that it was a relatively mild Israeli summer. Later I was hungry (band switch), frustrated (band switch), jealous (band switch), and tired (band switch). At one point I just stopped switching the band and told people to assume that I had switched it for the maximum number of times on that day.

Here's the interesting thing. Looking back, I am quite sure that I loved absolutely every minute of that trip. Each day ended with me feeling joyful, spiritual, connected, and grateful. So why all of the complaining and gossiping? After a long period of evaluation after the trip, I've decided that I was addicted to negativity. I'm also not alone in that many of the women on the trip confessed to constant wristband switching.

Many of us are just used to being negative. Complaining is as habitual as reaching for a cigarette or junk food and in many ways, equally as dangerous. Negativity pulls us out of the moment. It steals our energy. My negativity and complaining on that trip forced me to regroup in order to get focused on what was truly the opportunity of a lifetime. If I was complaining on this fabulous trip, how much must I be complaining in my day-to-day life?

After I got home, I went on an optimism hunt and realized that it wasn't actually that hard to find. I looked for good in my world versus bad. I looked for forgiveness and grace versus criticism and judgment. Every time I reminded myself to do so, my mood and my energy dramatically increased and I felt younger and more playful.

When I am complaining and negative, I only see the negative around me. When I am hopeful and optimistic, I only see the good. A client recently said to me that it's her voice she has to change and not so much her surroundings. How brilliant is that realization?

When we change that negative voice, we change the world. We change our world. Like any other addiction, this one has been hard to break and takes near constant vigilance but trust me, it's worth it.

It could be the most important work you ever do.

CHAPTER 11

Seen and Heard

We all have the need to be seen and heard.

What do you think my clients most frequently tell me they want from loved ones? It's to be seen and heard.

They want to be understood, listened to, loved, and accepted. Why do so many of us feel as if we are not seen and heard? One reason is because the world is filled with pretty dreadful listeners. People may be well intentioned, yet they are self centered and focused on their own agenda.

The other reason is that often we put people in our lives that duplicate what we are used to, even if we don't like it. If you had parents who didn't really see and hear you, then you were used to that type of behavior and maybe continue to attract people who are similar.

It's relatively common to do so, but it's also relatively unenjoyable. My clients are always surprised when they realize they are stuck in a pattern of finding people who can't really see them and hear them. So what are we to do to break out of this miserable pattern?

First, we need to see and hear ourselves. We need to have insight into who we are, what we want, and the people we want in our lives. Then we have to look in new places for "see-ers" and "hear-ers". (I think I made those words up.)

If you've met all of the same type of people in the same places, maybe it's time to go somewhere else. Not everyone in our lives will be able to see and hear us in a healthy way. But if we find one or two people who are able to do that, life will be so much better.

Here's another way to find "see-ers" and "hear-ers"; become that way yourself. Start to really listen to people. Be observant about who they are and what they are trying to share with the world. Validate those experiences for them and watch how profound it is when we do this for another. Soon enough, they will either be paying you back or you will start to attract other people who really want to get to know you.

Pay attention to your interactions. Notice how you treat yourself. (Re-read all the above chapters if you need to.) When you see and hear yourself, and do so for others, you will begin to find yourself with people in your life who do that for you.

You will indeed know that you are seen and that you are heard.

CHAPTER 12

Have An Opinion

*When you find your voice,
you have something to say.*

When I first started my coaching business, many people told me to be very careful about my opinions. "Don't talk about politics, religion, etc. You might alienate some people." Their advice was well intentioned but it really didn't work for me.

I'm a women's empowerment coach. I help women to find their voice in life, in business, and most especially for themselves. I help them to ask for what they want, to prioritize themselves, and to be assertive in all areas of communication. What kind of role model would I be if I didn't show them that I'm willing to have an opinion?

Admittedly, saying what's on my mind is sometimes scary for me. I still want people to like me. I'm a true people pleaser and it pains me when someone isn't pleased with me. Sharing an opinion is the easiest way to make others unhappy with you!

Yet, how can women support each other, support those that need their help, and advocate for themselves if they don't have a voice?

They can't and that's why I'm willing (even when it really scares me) to open my mouth and share an opinion, or defend someone else, or even to disagree. I try to do it kindly and without cruelty but I won't back down from doing it.

I've lost a couple of friends this way. I've probably lost a few potential clients or job opportunities yet I wouldn't change it for the world. When women are silenced in any aspect of their lives, they are no longer in charge of their own destiny. I refuse to sit back and let that happen.

I strongly encourage you to find your voice and to use it. Use it for yourself, for your family, for your community, and for the greater good. It's ok to disagree and it's ok to say no. Empowering ourselves can only happen when we do so.

Having a voice is not for the faint of heart! Be ready for people to call you bossy, bitchy, pushy, etc. It's guaranteed that a few people who enjoyed walking all over you are not going to be happy with this turn of events. Be kind, be compassionate, listen to others but never, ever lose your voice in the process. It is the most powerful gift you have so don't let it go to waste.

Let the chapters in this book give you the fuel to get started and also to replenish you when you need a pep talk. Find other women who are willing to speak up. You will. The more you exercise these lessons here and attract others who know what it's like to be seen and be heard, you will be in company where using your voice and voicing your opinions is the norm.

Now isn't that a wonderful world to be a part of?

CHAPTER 13

Back to School—Grown Up Style

Be a lifelong learner.

Back to school time is a milestone each year when children head back to the classroom another year wiser and prepare for another long stretch of learning and growing. But what about adults? Are we done with school?

We may be done with classrooms, but we are never done learning. So many of us seem to be stuck in our old ways, having stopped intent learning years ago, and feeling as if our growing days are behind us. Wrong!

Why are we so willing to give up the joy that comes with being challenged to learn something new, to struggle, to study, to gain knowledge and abilities in new areas?

How about this year (and every year) as the children head back to school, you take on a new learning challenge for yourself? Learn a new language, a skill, a hobby, or an athletic achievement. Why not set a goal for yourself to accomplish something new, fabulous, and to learn something that you've always wanted to learn? Start today by thinking about what you want to learn and then decide how you are going to go about doing so.

Do you need to get more information, sign up for a class, find some reference material, or find someone to take on this challenge with you? Get to it! Do it today and take on the joy and challenge that comes with learning something new.

Here are a few ideas: read a book that is really challenging for you and set a daily page goal; write a blog or article on something that you really care about; start running; take up yoga; start to learn a new language; or take a class on something you know little about.

There is a never-ending list of ideas and ways to grow and learn. Hopefully something you glean from these pages will spur you on to want to learn more. Take yourself "back to school" and find the growth and the joy that comes from being a lifelong learner. Your happiness and confidence will grow exponentially as you do so.

CHAPTER 14

A Radical New Way to Build Your Self-Esteem

It's time to be comfortable in your own skin.

In my search for my own self-esteem and well-being, I've met so many women who seem to be struggling with these issues as well. Rarely do I hear a woman say that she is comfortable in her own skin, confident in her abilities, and impervious to the criticisms of others. Some have one of those three conquered, but it seems rare to have all three.

Why are we blind to our beautiful qualities? Why are we so able to see our faults yet turn a blind eye to the qualities that make us strong, happy, and beautiful? Why don't we see what those who love us see?

I'm not sure that I have the answer, yet I do think that as women hit puberty there does seem to be a self-esteem drain that continues throughout adulthood. I think media and advertising play a role, but I think it's bigger than that as well.

Building our self-worth and self-esteem is not a one-ticket endeavor yet maybe if we start with one small change, it will lead to bigger and better strides.

Here's my radical idea: how about you start to believe it when someone says something nice to you. When someone says, "You look nice today," believe them. When they tell you that the project you did was wonderful, believe them. Thank them without diminishing their compliment. When someone praises your children or your parenting, own it!

I wouldn't have to convince you to own the negatives, so why do I have to pitch it to you that the positives might be true as well? Maybe you are as great as people tell you you are. Maybe it's all true! Believe it.

What would happen if you accepted their words and took them in as little shots of happiness to your soul?

What have you got to lose?

Take compliments from a stranger and tally them as fact. When a loved one compliments you, that should count as double. When you compliment yourself or recognize your own amazing qualities, that's priceless.

Start today; start right now. You are wonderful. Even if I don't know you, I know that you are wonderful. It's time to be wonderful and to believe that we are too.

Stop deflecting compliments and start owning them. You will see your confidence increase.

CHAPTER 15

Put On Your Lipstick and Face the Day

*Your track record for getting through
bad days so far is 100%.*

I posted a meme on Facebook that said, "On particularly rough days when I'm sure I can't possibly endure, I like to remind myself that my track record for getting through bad days so far is 100% and that's pretty good."

I didn't make up that statement and I don't know who did, but I really like it. It sums up what I tell my clients and my belief in how strong and courageous they are.

One client recently asked me, "Why do bad things happen to me?" There are all kinds of answers I can give her about the law of attraction or looking for the good in even the bad times, but I don't think that will help her right now. I'm not sure any words will, but I did remind her that she has survived other bad times and gotten herself up and out of those times to do wonderful things for her and her family.

For me, knowing that is often what gets me through the rough patches, knowing that I will get through those days and better days await me. As the saying goes, this too shall pass.

Another client who is going through a very challenging time texted me the other morning with this, "I'm getting up, putting on my lipstick, and moving forward." I wanted to frame those words and hang them in my office to remind me and others that that's really all we can do. Get up, put on your lipstick, and face the day.

Keep moving, look for happiness, find comfort and love wherever you can, and don't give up. Interestingly enough, my lipstick-wearing client got some good news later that day. My "why do bad things happen to me?" client took a break from her stress and prayed and later that day she got some much needed good news as well.

So what can you do on those tough day? Lipstick, a prayer, a walk, a treasured book, your favorite music, your best friend? What helps you get through it? Sometimes it is just getting up and moving through your day. Sometimes "heavier equipment" is needed such as chocolate or a glass of wine or getting a massage, but there is always something that will help you get through that challenging time.

Happiness truly awaits you on the other side of the challenge. Sometimes it is because you plowed through the challenge and sometimes simply because there is plenty of happiness to be found.

Recently I was at a women's event and was asked to think of something that symbolized the motto of my life. I ended up choosing the infinity symbol because my mantra has always been, "I never give up" and the infinity symbol reminds me of that continuous movement.

My family doesn't always like the side effects of that mantra but it has served me well in that when I'm at my lowest I say to myself, "You never give up and you won't now." So I don't and I put on my lipstick, I say a prayer, I kiss my kids, walk my dog, and I continue my 100% track record of getting through bad days. You will too.

CHAPTER 16

Facing Fears and Finding Joy

What did you want to be when you grew up?

I wanted to be an author. Books were my joy, my escape, my adventure, and my friend when things got tough.

As I got older, slowly my dream of becoming an author faded as I took on the "have to's" and "shoulds" that seem to come with growing up and fitting (comfortably or not) into society. I went to college, got married, had kids, and though greatly enjoying all of that, felt that something was missing.

A few years ago I told my oldest son that I wanted to write a blog. It was the first time that I spoke out loud about my dream of writing. It took me another couple of years to finally gather the courage to write that first blog post. I wrote about women who put off their own dreams in order to make sure others reach theirs.

I was terrified to post that blog. What if people hated it? What if they liked it? What if they talked about what a bad writer I was behind my back? Those and countless other worries almost kept me from hitting send. Yet I also kept saying to myself, "So what if others don't like it? I can live through that."

I published that blog and my friends really liked it (or at least they were gracious enough to say so). Since that time I've written many blogs to highly mixed reviews and comments. I've lived through all of it and woke to write again. (And here I am with a book.)

I once happened onto a rather terrifying opportunity to throw my blog into the mix on the "Momastery" web site. Momastery is an outrageously popular blog in which the author Glennon shares her truths about life, family, marriage, and religion. I highly recommend it.

After applying for the event and receiving the posting instructions, I wrote my blog, rewrote my blog, hated my blog, corrected my blog, and eventually accepted my blog and prepared to post it. Yet when I went on the website ready to share it with Glennon's hundreds of thousands of visitors, I saw that HUNDREDS of other bloggers had already posted their wonderful words. HUNDREDS! I couldn't compare to them. I wasn't worthy of posting my little bathing suit blog amongst these amazing manifestos. Surely I would be exposed as the writing fraud that I am.

Yet my naturally (and annoying to many, mostly my children) stubborn nature won that day and my blog was posted for the world to see. I'm not sure how my writing stacks up to the others and I've realized that it really doesn't matter. Because I WRITE! I write, I write, I write!

I do that one thing that I had always dreamt of doing. The little girl with her nose in a book has written words on a page and even if no one else likes them, she wrote them. The woman who wrote that blog knows that doing something she loves to do makes her more joyful, more energetic, and more optimistic than she would be otherwise.

What is it for you? What makes your heart sing? It might make you nervous too, but you know that the joy outweighs the fear. Deep down, you know that. As always, I urge you to face your fears and do that one thing that you have always dreamt of doing. Joy and happiness wait for you on the other side, whether you do that one thing well or not.

Fear is in our heads and the worst case scenarios can never be worse than giving up on our dreams. Never.

Before you read another page in this book, decide what that joy is for you. Promise yourself right now that you will go for it. I would love to hear your stories! (My contact information is in this book. Reach out and share!)

CHAPTER 17

The Mean Girl and The Bathing Suit

Stop being the mean girl in your life.

Here's the blog I mentioned above.

Since I was young, a mean girl has viciously bullied me. She criticizes my appearance; she is condescending, rude, and terribly cruel. The mean girl tells me that I'm stupid, I should give up, and that my ass is too fat and my legs are too bumpy. She's criticized my ability to parent, to be a wife, a friend, and a daughter. She has even chastised me endlessly on the days that I don't get my dog out for a walk. The mean girl, however, is at her most wicked when I go bathing suit shopping. It's a feeding frenzy for her in which she throws out one horrid criticism after another.

The mean girl of course is me. Yet she feels oddly like another person because I'm not really a mean girl. I don't criticize others, particularly not on their appearance. I'm generally and genuinely kind and compassionate except when it comes to me.

The mean girl has bullied me my whole life and she was there even in the days when I was looking young, thin, and sans cellulite. There is no pleasing her and thus she has held me back in more ways than I'd like to admit. I'm afraid of her and I'm afraid of what she will say to me and how I will feel when she's done.

Because of the mean girl, I have avoided doing things that I love, been fearful of saying and asking for what I want, played small when I really wanted to play big, and put a nice hard shell around myself that kept me from loving more freely and with less fear.

A few years ago I hit the limit with the mean girl. It was time for her to go or at least to shut up. I got more assertive with her and walked past her when she was spewing her nastiness. All aspects of my life started to improve as I stood up to my bully.

All aspects that is, except for my appearance. The mean girl sent me flying out of an exercise class because of her relentless judgment and comparison to the other women in the class. She had me in tears in countless dressing rooms as I tried on clothes but left empty handed and emotionally drained. I just couldn't seem to get a handle on holding her off when it came to my weight and body image.

Recently I had to do the dreaded bathing suit shopping because my previous suit had become threadbare. It was that oddly decent bathing suit that hid an assortment of flaws yet didn't feel as if I was wearing a girdle. I cried when I had to get rid of it. The mean girl has never let me shop for bathing suits without her and therefore most of these outings end with me in tears, calling myself names, and vowing to lose 20 pounds within the next hour.

I desperately wanted this trip to be different so I decided that I was going to drown out mean girl's voice with nicer words of my own. Entering the bathing suit store I began the internal mantra of, "Be kind, be kind, be kind." As I picked out a few suits I started to mutter the mantra quietly to myself.

I went into the dressing room and as I started to try on the first suit I could feel mean girl headed my way. "Be kind, be kind, be kind," I said in a louder and louder voice. The sales girl knocked on the dressing room door to check on me but I just continued with my mantra, which at this point was near yelling.

The first couple of bathing suits were rather dreadful and mean girl was circling me, ready to give me the, "Hey fatty, you can't wear a bathing suit. Do they sell tents in this place?" Yet I wouldn't let her in and by the last suit I tried on (in black of course), I was able to look at myself in the mirror and say, "That looks nice."

Still in shock that I had even complimented myself in a bathing suit, I was sure at that point that I had won; I beat the mean girl off and was never to be bathing suit bullied again. I carried my rather high priced new swimsuit to the cash register feeling relatively proud and confident.

Just as I put my suit on the counter I felt mean girl's presence. This had always been her favorite moment in the past, to make nasty comments about me to the salesperson and to point out the size of my new swimsuit to the other size 0 customers. I started to sweat just waiting for her to say, "Yep I'm buying the baby elephant size again." Or, "I'm just a good lunch away from having to shop at the muumuu store."

I steeled myself for the worst when the cashier asked if my nice black bathing suit would be all for me today. I could feel the mean girl near me, could sense her desire to tear me down but I wasn't going to lose to her this time. I kept thinking, "Be kind. Be compassionate. Love me no matter how I look. Accept me as flawed yet beautiful."

The mean girl seemed to hesitate and then she looked at the cashier with a diva look, tipped her head back, flipped her hair and with the most confident voice I've ever heard said, "No, I'll take it in hot pink too."

CHAPTER 18

4 Bold Ways to Love The Way You Look

Sweetie, it's time to LOVE what you see in the mirror.

In my blog, I have written on body image and learning to like our own appearance and our bodies. In this book on happiness and confidence, a dose of that seems appropriate here, especially as a follow up to my bathing suit story.

In a perfect world I would never have to write this section because we would all live shame free, content in our own skin, and rock perfect confidence in how we look.

Sadly, we don't live in a perfect world and women swim in a sea of mixed messages every single day. Ultimately, all of those messages are shame inducing in that women just can't seem to win ... no matter what we do. And it seems few of us feel truly happy with how we look.

Whether we like it or not, appearance matters, both in our society and quite honestly, to a lot of us personally. Is it even possible to actually love the way we look?

I think so. And, here are my tips to help you get there:

1.Remember a time you felt truly good about yourself.

You felt comfortable in your own skin and happy with what you saw in the mirror. What was it about that time that created those feelings? Was it what you wore? How much you weighed? Or, was it how you were living your life at the time?

Ask yourself if it is realistic to get back to a similar place. Certainly we can't turn back our age and often even our weight (at least in the short run) so we may have to find other ways to love our appearance. Remind yourself of what brought you happiness at that time and how that happiness led to your confidence in your appearance.

If you don't ever remember a time that you felt good about yourself, then you get to start with a clean slate! Think about recent days in which you felt energetic and happy with how you moved through your day. Did you eat better on those days? Get a good night sleep? Exercise?

Studies show that more time in front of the mirror actually leads us to feel worse about ourselves. So think of how you felt about your appearance without overly focusing on the mirror or pictures.

2. Focus on wearing flattering clothes, not the latest fashion.

Some of the trendiest fashions aren't right for everyone. If it doesn't fit well and feels uncomfortable, don't wear it. Nothing makes me feel worse about myself than too tight clothes, or styles that just don't *feel* right on my body.

I'm the most confident when I wear things that fit my body shape well and allow me to feel comfortable and energetic throughout the day. This doesn't mean excessively baggy or matronly styles, but rather clothes that you slip on and you feel just right in them. Attractive yet comfortable.

Please don't get caught up in size anxiety! Trying to fit into a one size down dress only makes you miserable, both in the dressing room and moving through your day. The size is irrelevant if you feel comfortable and confident in your clothes.

3. Shift the nitpicking b*tchy voice to a gracious and loving one.

If you look in the mirror and say the following to yourself, "OMG, you look fat in that. Your hair is dry, frizzy, and ugly. You have zits. Your eyes are too close together!" not only are you acting like a nitpicking bitch but you are also training your brain to look for the negative.

What if you looked in the mirror and found something kind to say to yourself? What if you actually looked for the good instead of the bad? Science states that finding the good instead of bad will reduce, both stress and the negative feelings you have for yourself.

4. Stop judging other people's appearance.

Here's the bottom line, if you constantly notice and comment on other's appearance, you're clearly struggling with those issues yourself. Judging others is ultimately judging ourselves. If someone is too fat, too thin, too ugly, too pretty, then we're possibly those things ourselves.

If how you relate to the world relies on how you and others look, you are in for a very rough ride. As we learn to start seeing the beauty in others, we begin to find it in ourselves. Start looking for good qualities in yourself and the people in your life. Those qualities will lead you to loving how you look regardless of a bad hair day.

I feel most beautiful on the days that I am helping others, focused on my work, and doing things to take care of myself. The mirror can never give me that type of confidence.

You are in charge of how you feel about yourself. Set your own appearance terms and set them realistically and with compassion. Adopt a health and wellness plan that feels right for you so that you feel good and thus look good. Find a look and feel that are right for you and then love the way you look because of the way you feel.

The size of your thighs or the shape of your lips can only look good to you if choose to see them as beautiful. If you let the world dictate whether you are beautiful or not, you are likely to end up disappointed in your appearance.

When you're in charge of your own vision of beauty, you can truly love the way you look.

CHAPTER 19

I Feel Sexier at 50 Than I Ever Did at 25

You can love who you are today.

Since turning 50, I've felt surprisingly peaceful about myself and my appearance. I hear women my age complain that they miss being 25. They miss their pre-pregnancy figures, but not me.

Here are some reasons why I love my (totally sexy!) body more today than ever before:

1. I didn't love my 25-year-old body.

I was constantly unhappy with my weight, what size I wore, how I compared to movie stars and models. I look back and laugh at how much I ate and how relatively thin I was despite my very unhealthy diet. I felt nowhere near sexy.

Is it inevitable that we are never happy with our appearances, no matter how fit and how youthful we are? Maybe if

I had my 50-year-old mind attached to that younger body, I would like it more but I doubt it. I've finally found some body acceptance and I don't plan on giving that up.

2. This body of mine has provided me with a wonderful life so far.

I have three beautiful children that kept residence in this body for 40 weeks each. I was blessed with healthy pregnancies, the ability to breast-feed and strength enough to schlep three babies around.

This body allows me to walk, run (if I choose), ride a bike, get from Point A to Point B by skipping if I want. My body is the vehicle that I take with me everywhere and I do not want to take it for granted.

3. I'm much less focused on my appearance (which happily opened up a lot of time in my schedule).

Honestly, I think I have a few extra hours a day that used to be spent obsessing over how I looked, what I would wear to the next big event, exercising more than necessary, and thinking about or following some low calorie diet.

I still exercise and I still manage to put some vegetables in my mouth, I just stopped worrying about it so much. My mind is happily free of counting every calorie or fat gram and has opened up to plotting how women can take over the world. And that's sexy!

4. I finally trust that those who love me do so for a whole lot more than how I look.

I have a husband who loves me, my children love me, my friends are as loyal as ever, my parents haven't disowned me and my dog greets me as if I am the most beautiful woman in the world.

It appears that I have surrounded myself with people who don't much care about my 25-year-old body or my 50-year-old body, so why should I? Oddly enough, I've never felt more comfortable in my own skin, and I'm pretty sure that's what people see when they look at me.

So, as you age (and if we are lucky, we all do), I recommend you look back to that 25-year-old you, not with regret, but with joy. 25 was wonderful but so is 50 and beyond.

Isn't it time to stop fighting with your appearance and start enjoying your life?

CHAPTER 20

The Secret of Happiness Is Surprisingly Easy

You know now the one true secret of happiness.

With most things in life, we make it so much harder than it has to be. What is the one true secret of happiness? It's surprisingly easy and yet often difficult for most of us to achieve. The true secret of happiness is to find your passions and to follow them throughout your life.

Close the book. My work here is done.

Seriously, when we are unhappy, we have fallen off the path of what means the most to us. What do we value most? What are we doing when we feel happiest, in the groove, the most energetic and joyful? If you know what that is and you aren't doing it, I'm guessing you aren't very happy.

Allow your passion to transport you to your happy place. Passion comes when we get into that space where time just stops and we flow into what we are doing seamlessly. Some people call it the zone. What activities or pursuits do that for you? It can be a physical pursuit or an intellectual one. It can be emotional or spiritual but whatever it is, it absolutely transports you to your really happy place. So why aren't we all doing this? Why are we not following our passions?

It seems we've learned to negatively judge what we value most. One of my clients absolutely loved being home after school and hanging out with her kids but felt guilty because she "should" be doing something else. Once she realized that her passion was her kids and she allowed herself to simply enjoy that time, she started to feel happy and content.

Another client thought that she should spend every moment entertaining or connecting with her children and thus have little time for her own passions. Once she allowed herself to get over the guilt and read a book or talk to a friend, she felt so much more fulfilled and less anxious about her children.

Your passion or purpose is unique to you, valuable beyond measure, and the true secret to a happy life. If you don't know what that is, start looking for it by noticing what you are attracted to throughout your day and week. Stop judging yourself and worrying about what others think and start pursuing what you love. Have you always wanted to write, ice skate, dance, help others, start your own business or even sing in front of others? Then find a way to add it to your life right now and bring on the happy dance!

CHAPTER 21

The Happiness Hunt:
The External Pursuit

*Many people look for happiness
in all the wrong places.*

One of the most common reasons that women come to see me is that they have lost the feeling of happiness in their lives. Maybe life didn't turn out the way they thought it would or maybe it did and they thought they would be happier. Or they have lost weight, or finally have a family, or have gotten divorced, or finished college, and yet the happiness is still missing. They are joyless and without energy and just don't know where to begin.

And that's where my work comes in because I think most of us are looking for happiness in all the wrong places. Happiness can be found with external things such as a new car, clothes, weight loss, etc., but not always. Happiness can also be found internally by shifting our focus, expressing our feelings, understanding our responses, and connecting to our true values. Yet most of us have no idea how to achieve happiness either externally or internally.

Let's focus on the external pursuit of happiness and next chapter I'll talk about the internal pursuit.

It may sound crazy, but most women don't know what makes them happy. Despite outward appearances of having it all pulled together and pretending happiness, many women say that they aren't very happy. Why would this be?

I find that most of the women who come to me don't know what unique factors make them happy. Maybe so many of us have been sold an external picture of happiness that we've lost contact with what really works for us. Some of us just want a safe car, others an attractive car, and some don't want a car at all because it's too expensive and they prefer to walk. Yet a lot of us seem to follow a prescribed path to happiness whether it's a car or not and don't really consider if it's right for us personally. You get the point I'm making.

Why not begin to connect with the outward items that actually bring happiness and value to your life. Yes, it is that simple. Connect with the things that make you happy. Do you like an organized, clean living space? Do you like comfy couches or fuzzy blankets? Do you need better lighting or a new laptop?

Check in with yourself on both material and non-material external issues and figure out what suits you so that you start to feel contentment and joy because of your external world. Do you wear high heels because you think you look good but they feel terrible? Or do you prefer dresses to pants? There is no right or wrong way to be happy. Each of us must look to and find our own way to get there.

Start noticing today when you feel joy, when you feel irritable, and when you feel calm and steady. Just notice, don't judge. Then begin to think about what you can change and what you can't.

Start making small changes that feel good to you, make them a part of your daily life. It takes a little bit of effort to be happy but it takes a lot of conscious awareness about what happiness really means to us.

I help women learn exactly what's keeping them from being happy and we design a happiness plan specifically for them. You can get started now by noticing what in your external world brings you joy and happiness. To continue on your happiness hunt, jump right in to the next chapter.

CHAPTER 22

The Happiness Hunt (Part 2): The Internal Pursuit

It's what's going on inside that matters.

We discussed the external factors of joy and happiness, those things outside of us that light us up. It is good to reach out for more of what we want and let go of what we don't want. Now let's talk about the important path to happiness that is our internal process that leads us there.

Joy, fulfillment, and happiness can happen despite external situations that are difficult. Can we be happy if we don't like our job or if we don't live where we want to or if our car breaks down? Can we find contentment in our lives even if we have had tragedy strike, or difficult childhoods, or a change in life that we didn't want? The answer is yes and that comes from the internal process of changing our mindset.

How do we do that? What if we are miserably unhappy because our spouse is leaving us or are children aren't doing what we want them to do? We actually need to choose to look at these situations from a different angle.

We have to ask ourselves what exactly we can control and then choose to let go of the rest. Almost always we have no control over what others do, think, or say, so letting all of that go is the very beginning of finding happiness in our lives. This doesn't mean that we don't acknowledge our feelings and allow ourselves to grieve, cry, and get angry if that's what we need. It does mean that we acknowledge and allow those feelings and then when we are ready we choose to allow the feelings of happiness and fulfillment to be our focus.

That is really important. Read that again: We choose to focus on feelings of happiness and fulfillment. Your happiness is directly correlated to what you focus on.

Happiness is a byproduct of finding meaning and purpose in our lives. When we can't control circumstances, we can control how we perceive everything that is going on around us. Looking for meaning can help us come to terms with loss and change and allow us to look for the silver lining in those situations.

When we actually seek joy, we find it easier than if we look for the bad in all situations. Happiness can come from the smallest changes that we make in our thinking. Our thoughts are what lead to our feelings so if we change our thoughts we will change how we feel.

Maybe our children are growing up and becoming independent and we are feeling sadness for this change. If we think to ourselves, "I am sad that my children are growing up and that they won't need me as much," then we will feel sad and disappointed at that change in our life.

If, on the other hand we think "Although I am sad that my children will be leaving my home, I am grateful to have had them at all and to have raised them to be independent and self sufficient." In the second scenario, we acknowledge our sadness but we look for the silver lining of happiness in that part of our lives. Our thoughts will lead to happier feelings of contentment and pride. We can always look for the silver lining of happiness in every situation.

The key to the internal path to happiness is to change your brain functioning from old negative messages to new, more positive versions. How do we do this? Practice! Every time you hear yourself think something negative, stop yourself, notice it and think about a new thought that you can replace the old one with. It doesn't have to be fancy or detailed; in fact, something along the lines of "All is well" will work just fine.

Keep saying it and thinking it until you have carved a new brain pattern of positivity and your feelings of happiness will follow. This truly is the key to the internal path to happiness.

Here's an exercise that can help you. A few years ago on January 1st, I started to put a small entry into a "One line a day" journal. I wrote something short each evening about my day and what worked in that day and what didn't. My goal was to put more joy into my life immediately. Although from the outside looking in on my life, you might have thought I was doing pretty well, but inside I was miserable. I'd lost track of what I loved to do in life, I didn't feel creative, or productive, and I wasn't the mother, wife, or woman that I wanted to be.

That journal was the beginning of my "joy journey." I look back on the early entries of that journal and I can see the progress I have made. From the outside I don't look all that different; I haven't lost weight, changed my hairstyle, or beefed up my bicep muscles. In many ways, everything has stayed the same yet truly everything is completely different. I prioritized happiness and in doing so, I found just that.

So how did I do it? I got brutally honest with myself about what I enjoyed in life and what I really didn't. I let go of the crappy voice in my head that was always telling me I wasn't good enough and that I SHOULD be a different kind of mother, wife, or woman. There isn't a one size fits all life path so why are so many of us trying to fit into it?

I started to do the work that I love, that I know I'm good at, and that energizes me and gives me joy and also brings my unique gift to the world.

A huge game changer was that I stopped caring what others think. These days my house is messier, dinners are often sketchy, and I bought my family more underwear so I could do less laundry. I started to drop the perfection pressure and actually asked and allowed my family to join me in the running of our family home and the world didn't end. In fact, it got so much better.

I stopped caring what others thought and started to take risks that led to even more happiness. My family started to notice the change and the tension started to leave our house as the laughter and joy came in.

The joy journey started with one small step that I did each day. That small step led to more small steps and now the joy journey is part of my life.

What is one small step you can take today to start your joy journey? It can be something simple that you do for a few minutes each day such as playing your favorite song, reading, knitting, or taking a short nap. It can be taking something out of your day that makes you miserable or sucks the energy right out of you.

It all begins with your noticing. Start small. And watch the huge changes that occur.

CHAPTER 23

Three Best New Year's Resolutions

Any time is a new year and a place to start.

I started my journaling to joy exercise on January 1, but you can start any time. Do not wait until the year change rolls around to embark on your path to happiness. And when you do find yourself looking at a new calendar page and a new year, remember what you read here right now about New Year's Resolutions and change the way you do yours.

Each year on January 1, millions of women (and men) vow to lose weight. Apparently, only about 5% of them succeed for any length of time. From my observations, the ones that don't succeed spend the rest of the year obsessing about their weight and their lack of weight loss success.

How many more years of your life do you want to spend thinking about your weight, clothes size, number on a scale, or your next diet? What fabulous things are you missing out on because you've given so much of your energy to dieting?

Remember that your happiness is directly related to what you focus on. How about you focus on your joy? Your happiness? Your confidence? Your enjoyment of life!

Let these be your New Year's resolutions from now until the end of time:

One: Resolve to let others live their lives and you actually live yours.

If you hear yourself saying, "My kids are my life" "My dog is my life" "Food is my life," who is living your life? Apparently it is not you.

Let other people and things be in your life, and you go have one of your own. In case you forgot, you can't have much of a life if you are focused on food or lack thereof. Women, particularly mothers, seem to believe that others are more important than they are and thus get into the self sacrificing, miserable martyrdom loop. Don't do it. No one wins in this scenario. Live and let live.

Two: Do one thing a day that scares you.

This line from Eleanor Roosevelt is quoted often. I saw it on that very famous 21st century philosopher, the Lululemon bag. It's actually a brilliant idea and will most likely keep you from obsessing about your diet or your kids or whatever else you have been too wrapped up in.

It can also guarantee that you succeed in resolution #1. Living your own life can expand when you apply #2. What are you most afraid of? Asking for a raise, changing careers, working outside of the house, bungee jumping, writing your novel, dating, ending a relationship?

Whatever it is, this is the time. Nothing is as wonderful as moving past fear and finding that the other side is better than you could have imagined. Find your voice, conquer your fears, and you will find greater happiness and confidence.

Three: Figure out what makes you happy, fulfilled, and motivated, then do it everyday.

This is exactly what we have been talking about in our happiness hunt discussion. Sounds simple but must not be because most people aren't doing it. Women walk into my office weighed down with responsibilities, guilt, and overwhelm. Most of them haven't even considered living their own dream. For some reason they don't think they are worthy of it. That's BS! You will be a better partner, parent, friend, professional, and human being if you take care of your own needs.

So what is your dream? Why aren't you living it? All those excuses don't hold water anymore, do they?

What are you waiting for? Your "new year" starts now!

CHAPTER 24

Dealing with Guilt and Shame

The guilt/shame loop; are you stuck in it?

Although my clients come to me to talk about a lot of different issues, at the heart of our talks is a common issue that they are all struggling with. Guilt and shame.

I call it the guilt/shame doom loop. Here's what it looks like, "I overeat, I feel guilty and then I'm terribly ashamed of myself so I end up eating even more." "I got stressed, yelled at my kids, felt like crap, beat on myself and then yelled at my kids again." "I know I should be promoting my business but I feel so guilty because my business is doing well and my friend is going through such a bad time so I'm too ashamed to be successful."

There are lots of different versions of this story, but it all boils down to the same thing. For some reason we are most comfortable giving ourselves an emotional beat down and then hanging on to our feelings of shame and guilt. These feelings lead to lower energy levels, short tempers, and behavior that doesn't feel good.

Why is it so hard for so many of us to let go of guilt? Here's the deal with guilt: either use it to make some positive changes in your life or let it go! Hanging on to guilt can only hurt you and keep you from being better in all aspects of your life.

It's important to take responsibility for our actions but it's not necessary to hang on to our mistakes for longer than it takes to decide how to do it differently next time. We can't change the past but we can use the past to motivate us for the future. Guilt and shame are energy and motivation suckers. They keep us feeling weak, helpless, and hopeless. Is that really how you want to go through your day?

So here's what I'm suggesting: recognize when you are throwing yourself into guilt and shame. Stop the thought process and ask yourself why you are feeling this way. What's your thought process around the issue and is your thinking sensible and helpful?

If not, change it to something that is more beneficial and hopeful. Most likely you will have to do this many times in a row until your thinking starts to change to something more kind and more optimistic. Don't give up!

Changing your mindset from one of guilt to one of hope will change how you feel about yourself and others, how you motivate to change behaviors you don't like, and how you ultimately achieve your goals. My clients are plowing through this work like champions; you can too!

Notice your guilt in all the tiny ways it sneaks up on you. Some of my clients found they weren't enjoying the moments and events that are supposedly for the purpose of enjoyment.

Admittedly, I've been known to do the same thing. One of my clients pours herself a glass of wine and then berates herself for "needing" that class of wine. Another feels guilty for taking a break from her children, another criticizes herself for a creative versus academic use of her talent, and yet another dreads the dinner hour because there is just too much to do afterwards. One client feels guilty for not focusing on her "big goal" 24 hours a day and another for not magically changing her own client's lives in minutes.

I've been known to plop on my hammock and then get crabby after a delicious nap because I didn't "get enough done." It's all rather ironic when you step back and look at it.

Let's adopt a healthier perspective, shall we?

Sit down and enjoy every damn sip of that wine and that moment or don't have the wine at all.

It's like the piece of chocolate cake that we chow down in a frenzy and then hate on ourselves afterwards, when if we just allowed ourselves to periodically enjoy the glory of a good piece of chocolate cake, all would be well.

Why can't we let ourselves just enjoy the enjoyable? Why isn't time away from our kids to rejuvenate ourselves ok? Why can't we ever just do nothing and let that be fabulous? Why must every moment be productive, doing for others, change the world moments and are we so sure that wine, chocolate cake, hammock napping, and time alone isn't actually what we and the world need?

You really only have two choices; enjoy the enjoyable or don't do it. If you are going to make the enjoyable miserable, then don't bother.

Let's make t-shirts or bumper stickers: Enjoy the enjoyable. In fact, praise yourself for enjoying the enjoyable.

"Nuff said.

CHAPTER 25

Help Each Other Fly

*You will feel happier and more confident
when you help others do the same.*

"Your butt looks great in those jeans, I'm so jealous."
This is something my friend Stacy said to me. Naturally, I'm flattered and not just because of the compliment. I admire her because she is willing to admit that she's jealous. She doesn't hold back at all.

I realize that even though I don't often admit to it, many times I feel jealous of others. In fact, I'm ashamed to admit that I will silently search for a flaw in the person that I'm jealous of. Have you ever done that? I think that I'm not alone in these thoughts and feelings.

Another friend asked me recently why some of her friends don't seem happy for her success, won't compliment her, and seem to avoid her as she starts to fly. Unfortunately, I think it's for the same reasons that I look for flaws or am embarrassed to admit that I'm jealous.

The truth is that it can be hard to be happy for others when you aren't feeling so great about yourself. It just doesn't seem fair that they are more successful, happier, more attractive, lucky, gifted, etc. Their success seems to highlight those areas that we feel most insecure about.

Once you get over your own insecurities and unhappiness and start celebrating the success of others, you start to feel better about yourself. Being happy for others takes absolutely nothing away from you. You'll find that, in a curious way, it feels quite good to admit to your feeling of jealousy and insecurity. You can just be yourself and own how you feel and why you feel that way. When you start to feel genuinely happy for someone else you begin to want the same thing for yourself. This is what happens when you become friends with wonderful women like Stacy.

In reality, your friend needs to hear your compliments. She needs you to celebrate with her. We have all been that girl who felt ugly, insecure, unimportant or unloved. We have been that girl who grows up to be a woman who still struggles with fears and insecurities. Trust me, it took a lot for her to dive in and build that business, or start a new job, or get healthy, or quit smoking, or find a partner who is perfect for her. She has been scared and unhappy just like you. It will mean the absolute world to her for you to give her that compliment, to recognize her success, and to celebrate with her.

It's easy to tear others down to say, "Who does she think she is?" and similar mean girl type of insults. Is that who you really want to be? How powerful would women be if we stopped pulling each other down and instead found things to support in each other? How much better would you feel about yourself if you found something wonderful to compliment in the women around you? Wouldn't you want the same for yourself? And just think of the messages we would be sending our daughters if they watched us help each other fly.

I believe we can lift each other up and help each other to fly. Make a point to help boost the confidence of others around you. You will notice your own happiness meter go up.

CHAPTER 26

The Confidence Conundrum

You can build your confidence connection is 3 steps.

Here's what I hear from clients quite frequently: "I just don't have the confidence to do that. I'm scared."

I get that, and it's a normal emotion to have fear around new situations and challenging pursuits. Interestingly enough, most advice around confidence sounds very much like a Nike commercial, "Just do it." Yet really, if we could just do it, then we wouldn't be talking about confidence, right?

Although I realize that action increases confidence and inaction increases fear, pitching that concept doesn't seem to be particularly helpful and therein lies the confidence conundrum.

So how do I help my clients push through the conundrum and into the confidence connection? With three very specific and relatively simple steps.

1) They change their internal messaging.

Most of us have a running tape in our head that can often be very negative and holding us back. "Oh I couldn't do that. It's too scary. I'll fail again." If that is our messaging, we can't possibly step into our fears and become confident. Therefore, I ask my clients to pick a statement of confidence and to repeat it to themselves again and again until they actually start to believe it.

The statement might be as simple as, "I can do this" or "All is well." (Or like I told myself when bathing suit shopping: Be kind!)

Often I suggest that they write it daily and speak it as frequently as possible.

When we tell ourselves that we can't do something, our brain scans our environment to prove us right. The same process works by telling ourselves that we can do it and our brain looks for evidence of the positive type.

It's going to be hard to become confident if you keep telling yourself that you aren't. Start right this minute by picking up a confidence type statement and repeating it to yourself numerous times a day.

2) They take one teeny tiny step into confidence.

After they've worked on their internal messaging, then it's time to take a small step into confidence. I ask my clients to pick out a very small change that they can make in order to become more confident.

Sometimes it's asking for something different on a restaurant menu and sometimes it's contributing to a meeting. It really doesn't matter what it is, but it needs to be something that feels like a bit of progress.

What is one thing that you can do this week that would make you feel just a little bit more confident? Is it learning something new, standing up straight, speaking up, speaking louder, or asking for something?

3) They workout their confidence muscle daily.

After they've taken a small step, I push my clients to build on that small step. What are two things you can do each day to feel more confident? What's a bigger confidence goal for you? What's your biggest confidence goal and what will you need to do to get there?

Sometimes it's just getting out of bed and sometimes it's approaching a challenging situation. Keep reminding yourself of your confidence affirmation, especially when you start to feel fearful or anxious. Do not berate yourself if you don't do it; remind yourself that you are doing your best. Don't give up!

Start today by listening to what you are saying to yourself and how you can change that message into one that will lead you to both confidence and action. Once you get the hang of it, it becomes easier and easier to do.

Think back to a time when you felt confident about something. How did you get there? Can you follow those steps again? I know that you can! Make this confidence connection and let me know your progress!

CHAPTER 27

Working with Women

Women can indeed work well with other women.

Igive talks and workshop presentations to various groups of wonderful women (and men) and I love to teach around the topic of Executive Presence for Women.

There isn't a day that goes by that I don't hear some negative opinion about or to women. "She's so high maintenance." "OMG, she's so b-i-t-c-h-y." "Who does she think she is?" I rarely hear the same comments about men and surprisingly (or not), I most often hear such comments from women.

Yet when I put a small group of women in a room and ask them to support each other, magic happens.

I recall the first time I asked women at a workshop to be videotaped and critiqued on their confidence, assertiveness, presence, and speaking ability. They were obviously (and understandably) nervous and uncomfortable with the exercise.

Yet each woman got up, did her absolute best, and then openly received feedback from her classmates.

The feedback was given with kindness, compassion, and a true desire to help. I watched their confidence rise as these women supported and helped each other.

So here's my plea to you and all women: SUPPORT EACH OTHER!

Please, look for the good in each other, share kind words and give feedback from a place of kindness not judgment. Teach your children to do the same thing. Women face enough sexism and misogyny throughout the world. Why would we want to contribute to that?

Let's stop the mommy wars, the body shaming, the sexist jokes, and standing by when others are being judged and criticized. Let's rise together and help each other to be strong, confident, safe, and able to achieve our goals. Let's break the glass ceiling, end violence against women and demand equal pay for equal work. Let's do it together. Supporting each other is how we will grow and succeed in all areas of our life.

What can you do today to support another woman? Can you pick up her kids, drop off dinner, lend an ear or a hand? Can you give her feedback that will help in her career? Can you mentor a younger woman to help her get promoted? Be motivated to do more, to say more, and to help more.

I know without a doubt that when women work together, great work is accomplished.

CHAPTER 28

The Courage of Clients

You have more courage than you know.

When I first decided to stop providing therapy and start life coaching, I worried that I wouldn't be able to get as "deep" with clients because we would only focus on superficial issues. I couldn't have been more wrong.

My clients walk into my office or call me on the phone and allow me into their lives with such courage and conviction that I'm often in awe of their determination.

Opening up to a relative stranger, sharing dreams, wishes, fears and insecurities is not for the weak-willed. My clients plow through our work together and go take on the world each in their own unique ways. I always ask what brought them to me, what gave them the courage to make that first call and to reach out for help. The answer is almost always the same. "I was ready to do things differently."

Is that you? Every client has said that she knew it was time to make a change. Maybe it was to change her relationship. Maybe it was her career, her parenting style, or to reduce her stress. Each of them knew that enough was enough.

That's also when I made my own changes. When enough was enough and it was time to live a better life.

I wish I could take credit for the changes that my clients make, but I'm just a blissfully lucky guide in their journey. There are many, many days that I pinch myself. I get to work with amazing women. I learn so much from each of them. I grow a little bit from watching them grow and when they fly . . . it is a sight to behold. Sometimes I want to scream their names to the world and say, "Will you look at her go? She is glorious!"

That is why I am compelled to create this book for you. It is a taste of the lessons that all women need to hear. You may or may not ever work with a life coach, but you will work on your life. Use the nuggets in this book to propel you forward on your journey. You do indeed have more courage than you know.

CHAPTER 29

Fear

We all feel fear. It is normal. You are not alone.

Every woman I've ever met (myself included) has confessed that what most often holds them back in life is fear. Fear of the unknown, fear of success, failure, making a fool out of ourselves; fear of hurting others, or of even being more successful than others. All of these are reasonable fears but they aren't helpful in propelling us to lead the lives we want to live. So how do we get over our fears?

If you look at the women around you who are successful in any aspect of their life, you will see that all of them have overcome fear. The mother who has a child with special needs was afraid when her child was first diagnosed. The woman who has been promoted numerous times was afraid to ask for that first promotion. The marathon runner was afraid when she first tied on her running shoes. The politician in your community was afraid when she first started making public speeches.

We are all afraid of something. The key is to understand the fear and to ask ourselves if we can survive if that fear is realized. The special need's mom is afraid that she won't be able to help her child and that it will be too hard for her yet when she faces that fear she realizes that she can help both her child and herself. The woman with the successful career realized that the worst she could hear is no and that she'd be ok with that but she'd never get a yes if she didn't ask. Most of us will be just fine even if some of our worst fears are realized.

That's the thing about fear, it's here to protect us from really dangerous things but it's more of an annoyance for other areas of our life. So get really clear about what scares you, look at it closely and ask yourself if you can handle it if those fears are realized. Here's a hint, you can.

Push through one fear at a time, see yourself get stronger and then pushing past fear won't be so hard for you.

Look to those around you and be inspired and energized. We all have fear. And we all can succeed. It's your time.

CHAPTER 30

Your Power Circle

Create your own power circle.

When I look back over the past few years and the dramatic changes that I've made in my life, I try to think clearly about how I got here so that I can help others do the same. One of the biggest "secrets" to the changes in my life came from having what I call my power circle.

Your power circle is those people you surround yourself with who will lift you up. Here is a short list of who I think you should have in your power circle.

1. Optimists

They believe that the world is generally a good and wonderful place. They have faith in people, and growth, and change, and recovery, and hopefulness when things don't seem that way. They are the people who promise you that things will get better even when you aren't so sure of it yourself. Don't go for fake optimists but rather the real thing. Real optimists are realists and hopeful. They acknowledge the reality but seek to make it better.

2. A mentor

Find a mentor, someone who knows more than you do and who wants to help you succeed in an area of your life in which you might need a little help. A mentor doesn't necessarily have to be older but they should be a bit wiser than you in order to show you the ropes.

3. Friends who make you laugh

It's good to have a variety of friends but having one or two friends who make you belly laugh is really priceless. I'm blessed with a few of these friends and I can always count on them to say something so spot on funny that nothing else really matters. Life is really too short to be too serious, too often. Find some gigglers!

I'm assuming you will have other people in your life who support you but I think these three types of people make life a little more wonderful.

Who will you include in your power circle?

Overcoming Obstacles

There are obstacles in life. You can get over them.

Sometimes there are external obstacles that hold us back in our life, a lack of money, time, etc. However, more often the obstacles that hold us back are the ones that we put in our own way.

Do you often tell yourself that you aren't smart enough to do something? Not strong enough? Have you said you thought you are too old, too young, too busy, and any other limit that you can think of?

I've had clients tell me that they are too heavy to be a public speaker, too old to start a new career, too young to be believed by others, too dumb to learn computer skills, and not good enough at math to pass a statistics class. They were all wrong.

I knew it but it took some work to convince them of it. Here's the problem, if that's what they believed then they were not only sure to fail but they had set themselves up to prove themselves right.

What beliefs are you holding on to that are limiting you? How can you let go of those beliefs? First, ask yourself how true they really are. If you look at the examples above, you will see that none of them were really true. If your beliefs aren't true, then you can push through that belief and accomplish what you had once thought you couldn't.

The client that thought she wasn't good enough at math to pass a statistics class was me! I spent most of my life believing that I wasn't good at math and when I decided to go to graduate school, I knew that I would be taking numerous statistics classes. How did I break through my limiting belief? I asked myself for evidence that I wasn't good at math. Guess what? I didn't really have any.

Then I asked myself if I was capable of learning, of asking for help, and of pushing myself, and my answer to all of these was yes. It wasn't easy, I had to constantly convince myself that I could do it, but I did. You can too.

Check those beliefs at the door and push through to do the things that you have always wanted to do but had convinced yourself you couldn't. It is time to convince yourself that you can!

It's all part of the happiness and confidence equation. The more you realize what you CAN do, the happier and more confident you are.

Learn something new, challenge yourself, pass a statistics class, or apply for a job that you once believed you couldn't do. You won't regret it. In fact, you will love it!

CHAPTER 32

The 12x Formula

Remember this formula and go for it.

I read a statistic that people who eventually quit smoking for good have (on average) twelve previous failed attempts at quitting. Yes, an average of 12 times they tried to quit and failed. If they had given up on the first try based on the assumption that they had tried and failed, they would still be smoking today.

Many people tell me that they tried something, failed, and thus now know or assume that they can't possibly do it. "I can't lose weight. I've tried and failed." "I can't get along with my husband. I tried and failed." "I can't get that promotion because I asked once and they told me no." "I'm a bad mom because I tried to discipline my kids and they talked back to me so I gave up." These are just a few of the examples that I hear on a daily basis.

When my clients tell me that they can't possibly try again, I not only know that they can, but I also know that eventually they will succeed as long as they keep trying.

If you've tried to incorporate a healthy exercise plan to your life but have failed in the past, ask yourself why. What do you need to do differently to succeed in the future? Did you try the wrong exercise? Did you try to do too much exercise or activities that were too strenuous for you? Did you work out at a time of day that wasn't really great for you? Did you have the mindset of, "I hate exercising?"

There are so many reasons that it may not have worked out for you, but do you really want to give up on making that powerful change in your life? Don't assume that because you haven't figured it out yet, you won't. Think of the 12x formula and keep going. Try again. Try in a different way. Seek help in the form of advice or support. Even if you've tried 12 times, keep going. Ask more questions of yourself; analyze your mindset, your feelings, and how you show up to make these changes.

Anything fabulous or major that I've accomplished in my life hasn't come easy. I've failed so many times that I make those ex-smokers look like speed quitters! Yet I've trusted the process and I've gotten back up and tried again.

I've learned something powerful with each failure and it's put me on a path to succeeding in a different way, maybe even a way that I hadn't thought possible.

Keep the 12x Formula in your head and go out there and try again! I'd love to hear about your progress, so drop me a note and let me know your challenge and how you are doing. I know you can do it!

CHAPTER 33

Scared? So What!

Use the "so what" factor and forge on.

Most of my workdays are spent talking to women about their dreams and goals. We also talk quite a bit about getting stuck in a variety of aspects of our personal and professional lives. Almost always women get stuck because they are scared of some aspect of their dream.

We've talked about fear earlier in this book. Maybe it's the unknown that scares them, or the disapproval of someone else, or failing, or even succeeding. Sometimes women are afraid of the reactions of their loved ones and sometimes they are afraid of making fools of themselves.

All of these are normal fears, yet fears hold us back, keep us stuck, and generally make our lives rather frustrating. But it doesn't have to be this way.

Get really clear on what your fear is and then ask yourself, "So what?" First, you need to figure out what you are really afraid of. Dig deep. Is it social embarrassment, disappointing others, or fear of failure? Identify the fear and then ask yourself, "So what?"

Let's say your dream is to be an author but your fear is that people will make fun of your writing. So what? What is the worst thing that can happen if people make fun of your writing? You'll be ashamed or embarrassed? Will you die of shame or embarrassment? Not only will you not die from shame, you are actually more than likely to learn and grow from it and know that you can handle some embarrassment without the world coming to an end.

Almost always our fears are in our heads and not really reality based. So if we face them and we ask ourselves if we can live through the worst-case scenario surrounding our fear, we can almost always move forward and step into that fear.

Brain surgeons had to learn something new in order to become surgeons. Do you think they were scared? At some point they had to let the reward of becoming a brain surgeon outweigh the fear of actually harming a patient in order to become skilled at what they do. Luckily, most of us have fears that aren't life and death and thus pushing through them probably isn't as hard as brain surgery!

Figure out what your fear is, say "so what" to yourself regarding your fear, and go out and live that dream! It gets easier with practice. So the next time you have a fear (you will have a next time, they never just stop showing up), you will be able to face it with all the knowledge and power you are acquiring in these pages, and you will be able to face it and say, "So what!"

CHAPTER 34

Harnessing Your Internal Strength

*You've got it. Find and harness
your internal strength.*

So many women tell me that they feel as if they are just puppets on a string in their own lives. They do things for others, they react to what others want, and they lose track of themselves. They don't address their own needs and wants and thus end up feeling insecure, unhappy, and without motivation.

I get it. I've been there myself. I understand how it happens, but I also know how to get out of it and get to a place where you are in charge of your own life. You can live a life of contagious confidence and true-life leadership.

I can hear you saying, "But that's the problem, I don't have internal strength." Wrong. We all have internal strength, but we have to clear out the crud to actually get to it. What's the crud? There are two main types of emotional crud that zap your internal strength.

The first is feeling sorry for yourself.

It's normal, it's relatively natural but it's really not helpful. Allow yourself a moment to recognize that you are feeling sorry for yourself and then ask yourself this question, "How is feeling sorry for myself going to help me?"

Then take that question to the next level, "How can I pull myself out of this space? What can I control in this situation? If I can't control something (or someone), how can I change how I'm looking at it?"

Keep reminding yourself that self-pity will NEVER change your situation. You can't lead your life from that space—ever. You need to own the situation, your role in it, and how you can change it or change your perspective of it.

Don't give up on this. Keep fighting your way through it until you no longer feel sorry for yourself. If you can't do it on your own, get help!

The second type of emotional crud that keeps you from feeling and being strong is anger.

Although anger is a perfectly natural human reaction, it is actually a secondary emotion. That means that anger comes from another feeling such as shame, sadness, fear, etc. Holding onto anger without digging to its source and ultimately changing it is a recipe for misery. You cannot be assertive, powerful, and the leader of your own life if you are stuck in anger.

Stop and ask yourself where is this emotion coming from? Is it possible that you are embarrassed, ashamed, afraid, tired, or some combination thereof? Weed it out in order to reduce or relieve that anger.

Anger often leads to bad behavior that then often leads to regret or remorse. Get yourself out of that space before it gets too comfortable for you! Who wants to live their life in anger? Certainly not a happy and confident woman like you!

Once you get a handle on feeling sorry for yourself and anger as a secondary emotion, you can begin the process of owning and utilizing your internal strength. It's there; you just have to find it. When you aren't angry, you can listen to others but more importantly listen to yourself. Confidence arrives at your door when self-pity walks out. Kick it out now and start finding contagious confidence!

CHAPTER 35

The Kindness of Readers

Trust that kindness will always win.

Social media has been a wonderful way to bring people together, reconnect with former classmates, brag about your children and share more information than most people are actually interested in. I'm typically quite entertained by Facebook posts or tweets from clever, funny people.

Unfortunately, social media also attracts many who use it as a place to bully, demean, argue, rant, and complain. I've wisely hid or unfriended these people yet periodically a nasty Facebook post finds its way to me and that has led to some soul searching on my part.

One night a particularly vicious post caught my eye that misquoted and took out of context the words of a woman who was discussing victim blaming of women who had been raped. This woman had been raped herself and now courageously spoke out to support others. A misquote was now circulating and comments were made to make fun of this woman and label her as uninformed and stupid. It was dreadful and disturbing. I made the upsetting mistake of reading the comments. This is when my faith in humanity began to waiver. The comments were aggressive, sexually violent, racist, bullying, demeaning, and cruel beyond reason.

I sat back in my chair filled with anger and hurt, wanting desperately to lash back at the cruelty and judgment of people who seem so miserable and so ready to hurt others. But I refrained.

Then my 20-year-old son came into the room at just that moment. He looked at me with his young, innocent eyes and his delightfully optimistic, idealistic personality and said, "Mom, can you recommend some life changing books for me?"

I just stared at him and part of me wanted to say, "Don't bother. The world is a cruel, terrible place. People judge and hurt each other for no reason other than the pleasure they take from it. Arm yourself with the pessimistic, negative shield that most adults carry and empty that overflowing optimism glass of yours."

Happily, I didn't say this. Instead I decided to reach out to my friends on Facebook to ask them for their book recommendations. That's when the magic happened.

It was 10:00 at night and I'd assumed most people would be in bed, but the recommendations came in fast and furious along with supportive, loving comments.

Friends of friends responded, adult children responded, old college friends wrote special private notes with some of their favorite life changing books. The people who responded represented both political parties, most major religious groups, different races, and different ethnicities. No name calling, no disagreeing or condescension, just pure love of reading and sharing that love.

What was even more amazing was the list of books that they came up with. Books that shared kindness, self-awareness, love of man, humanity, religion, spirituality, poetry, and charity. None of the books taught hatred, bullying, humiliating others, criticism or condescension.

The books that changed their lives were thoughtful and insightful and led these people to behave in kind; to choose kindness over cruelty and compassion over hate.

Reading has always been my salvation through sadness, fear, anxiety, and boredom. I read to learn and to grow but also for the sheer joy and entertainment of it. Reading has opened my mind, helped me find empathy and compassion when I might not otherwise have thought to look for it, and has made me a kinder, more tolerant person.

In a moment that shook my faith in others, the kindness of readers reassured me that all is well and that beauty abounds in books and in real life.

Thank you dear people who unknowingly reached out that night to brighten my spirit and to share your very intimate recommendations with my son. I am forever grateful.

Below is the list of the books that changed lives and in so doing changed mine.

The Red Lion by Maria Szepes

The Gifts of Imperfection by Brene Brown

This I know by Susannah Conway

Wild by Cheryl Strayed

Bridge to the Soul by Rumi

The Alchemist by Paulo Coelho

A Return to Love by Marianne Williamson

The 4 Agreements by Don Miguel Ruiz

The Amazing Adventures of Kavalier and Clay by Michael Chabon

The Art of Racing in the Rain by Garth Stein

The Celestine Prophecy by James Redfield

A Child Called It by Dave Pelzer

Tuesdays with Morrie by Mitch Albom

The Way of the Peaceful Warrior by Dan Millman

11/22/63 by Stephen King

Your Money or Your Life by Vicki Robin, Joe Dominguez and Monique Tilford

Outliers by Malcolm Gladwell

There are no Children Here by Alex Kotlowitz

Waiting for Godot by Samuel Beckett

The Chosen by Chaim Potok

The Good Earth by Pearl S. Buck

The Mists of Avalon by Marion Zimmer Bradley

Body and Soul by Frank Conroy

Many Lives Many Masters by Brian L. Weiss

The Bible Code by Michael Drosnin

The Thinking Life by P.M. Fomi

Outwitting the Devil by Napolean Hill

Man's Search for Meaning by Victor Frankl

Case for Faith and **Case for Christ** by Lee Strobel

It's Here Now by Bhagavan Das

Into the Wild by Jon Krakauer

Think and Grow Rich by Napoleon Hill

Ami:The Child of the Stars by Enrique Barrios and Glen Strock

Shantaran by Gregory David Roberts

The Poisonwood Bible by Barbara Kingsolver

The Fifth Sacred Thing by Starhawk

Autobiography of a Yogi by Paramhansa Yogananda

I Ching or Book of Changes by Richard Wilhelm, Cary F. Baynes, Hellmut Wilhelm and C.G. Jung

Kisses from Katie by Katie J. Davis and Beth Clark

To Kill a Mockingbird by Harper Lee

Coach Yourself to Success by Talane Miedaner

On the Road by Jack Kerouac

The Catcher in the Rye by J.D. Salinger

Love in the time of Cholera by Gabriel Garcia Marquez

The World According to Garp by John Irving

Native Son by Richard Wright

Portnoy's Complaint by Phillip Roth

Forever by Judy Blume

Ordinary People by Judith Guest

The Magic of Thinking Big by David J.Schwartz

Your Best Life Now by Joel Osteen

15 Invaluable Laws of Growth by John C. Maxwell

After Visiting Friends by Michael Hainey

Inspiration by Wayne W. Dyer

(Any that you would like to add? Drop me a line!)

CHAPTER 36

Best Year Ever

We're not getting older, we're getting better.

It was the best year of my 50-year-old life. Most of the other years were really nice, but this one was a standout. I didn't lose a pound, didn't drop a clothes size, didn't win the lottery, didn't find a cure for cancer, didn't win the Nobel Peace prize, didn't change my relationship status, and I didn't run a marathon (not even a half marathon). My children did not cure cancer either, nor did they get perfect ACT scores, or athletic scholarships, they didn't invent a million-dollar app or get published in a world famous science journal.

If you were an outside observer, you might think that my family and I had a rather average year. You would be wrong.

I made some huge changes that affected every moment and every interaction that I had throughout the year.

Here are the things I *stopped* doing:

- **Focusing and beating on myself for aspects of my appearance**. I am done worrying about my weight, the wrinkles on my face, cellulite, and levels of muscle tone. I've probably wasted years on diets, excessive exercise, a number on a scale, and signs of aging. Bottom line, this is me and I'm fine with it.

- **Worrying about what others think of me**. It's just not my problem. If someone is unhappy with me, they can nicely come and tell me what it is. I stopped concerning myself with feeling embarrassed, fear of rejection, humiliation, etc. Those things happen regardless so why not just do my thing? Funny, it feels like I have lost 10 lbs. since I stopped worrying.

- **Judging others and myself**. I'm still working extra hard on this one but it is worth the effort. I realized that when I judge others, I'm usually doing it because I'm unhappy with some aspect of myself. I have a rule with all of my clients; I won't judge them and I won't allow them to judge themselves. It appears that many of us need to work on this.

- **Making my children's issues my issues**. A wise new friend said this to me, "My children are not my life, my children are in my life." How wonderful to let go of the burden of feeling everything your child feels, taking responsibility for each positive and negative thing they do, and the incessant worry about all aspects of their lives. It's been interesting to watch my children blossom in their own unique ways as I've stopped overwatering and obsessing about them. Surprisingly enough, my own life has been more fulfilled and joyous as a result.

- **Worrying that behind every joyful moment something bad is about to happen**. Why can't we just accept happiness for what it is? Why must we always worry about what's around the corner? Why don't we trust ourselves enough to know that we will manage whatever comes our way? Right now I'm happy and I'm happy that I'm happy so don't try and talk me out of it.

Here are the things that I *started* to do:

- **Faced my fears head on**. I shamelessly plugged my business, my successes, and my skills as frequently as I could and I'm still here to talk about it. What good is having a skill or a product that you know can help others yet be afraid to market it? I also found my voice and I used it to stand up for others and myself.

- **Said yes when no felt much more comfortable**. Every scary yes led to some of the most amazing opportunities I've ever had in my life. Each yes also introduced me to brilliant, wise, kind people who helped me face even more fears. Another smart friend told me that many years ago she decided to be a yes vs. a no person and she changed the course of her marriage and the quality of her life because of it.

- **Took responsibility each and every day for my own happiness**. If I don't like something and I can change it, I do. If I can't change it, I change how I look at it. If I hear myself saying, "He made me mad" or "She made me act this way," I know that I'm not owning my own feelings and I'm letting others do that for me. I find things to do each day that replenish me and I reach out to people who are like-minded, supportive, and loving. If I'm not happy, I only have myself to blame and I'm done beating on myself.

As I wrote that it was the best year of my life, I did so knowing that people I love might have been counting the seconds for the year to be over. Many of my friends faced hardships with illness, death of a parent or loved one, divorce (though I think for most of them this was good news), and most devastating of all, the loss of a child. At times during the year I felt helpless in my ability to improve their situations or to ease their pain. I wondered if feeling joy was disrespectful to their suffering. Yet I do understand that we feel happiness and pain and that in our lives we will have both.

Every year I will seek out joy and happiness as much as I can because I know it will ultimately sustain me when times get tough and when others need me to be strong.

It does not matter what birthday it is for you this year, implement these changes and you too will feel stronger every day.

CHAPTER 37

Herstory and Your Story

Strong women serve as inspiration for our lives.

I love a good rags to riches story, not in terms of financial riches, but the bigger picture riches of a life well lived, filled with things that mattered most to the storyteller.

My favorite stories are from women and I've happened upon some pretty amazing ones. I'm profoundly grateful for Herstory and the writers that share their most intimate moments.

These stories, however, have led me to wonder if some women never have their story. That at the end of their lives, they can't point to that one moment that changed it all and led them on a path of self improvement and pure happiness.

I'm worried that it's more common than not based on the unhappiness I often witness. The woman on her death bed who says, "I stayed in that abusive relationship" or "I devoted my life to caring for my children and all they ever wanted was my money" or the sad women who leave all of their money to their beloved pet who really doesn't have much use for millions of dollars. How does this happen and why?

I think I found some of the answers from reading the inspirational stories of HerStory. In every story I read, our heroine found her voice and used it. She ignored fear, shame, abuse, criticism, lack of support and she became passionate about some aspect of life that she felt she could contribute to.

JK Rowling, a nearly destitute single mother, found her imagination and fearlessly put it to paper. She changed the reading habits of a generation and happens to be one of the most philanthropic women on the planet. Chutzpah for sure. Anne Frank, despite all of the misery that the outside world forced upon her, refused to be a victim and her story affects millions of readers today. Helen Keller, Gabby Gifford, Hillary Clinton, Condoleeza Rice, Madeleine Albright to name just a few. One of my favorite quotes is from Madeleine Albright: *It took me quite a long time to develop a voice, and now that I have it, I am not going to be silent.*

There were other examples that were less dramatic for the world but more so for the writer. Mothers realized that they loved to work outside of the home and bucked a judgmental world and went to work. Women who wanted to work inside of their homes with their children nearby found a way to do just that and live their greatest dream.

Women went to school, left a toxic relationship, discovered those who needed an advocate, they wrote, prayed, sang, danced, exercised, taught, and in their own small way, changed our world for the better.

In life coaching, we call this the victim to victory story. That day that you wake up and say, "That's it! I will not live like this for one more minute." And you start the process of change.

I'm not sure if it happens when we reach our pain threshold, boredom, or just that unbelievably powerful voice that keeps saying to us, "You have a gift, share it with the world."

I worry for those who keep ignoring that voice and slowly drag themselves to a miserable grave without having expressed that special something that brings joy and unique happiness into their lives.

So what is your story? Who will you share it with and when? You don't think you have one? We all do; we just have to put down all of our fears, worries, and defensiveness to find out. No small task, I know.

Keep your eyes open, stay curious, drop the victim act because it only serves to maintain that status. Quit being angry and aggressive and instead open your mind to the possibilities. Stop being jealous and judgmental because it's not very attractive and will forever hold you back. Finally, be fearless, act as if you own the world and go get it. Because you truly do. What have you got to lose? (Besides Fido's inheritance?)

CHAPTER 38

Take On The World
One Fear at a Time

We can teach, and learn from, our daughters.

I once brought my daughter and her two besties (she will be so annoyed that I used that word) to work with me. My work for that day was giving three different presentations on bullying to grade school students, their teachers, and administrators at a local school. There were 200 kids in each group presentation.

I brought the girls with me because I'm terrified of speaking publicly to children even though I speak publicly for a living. If given the option to give a talk to 1,000 angry adults or 10 average children, I'd take the adults every time hands down. Kids are a tough crowd.

A majority of adults would tell you that they are terrified of speaking in public. There is a phobia named in honor of this fear, glossophobia. I'm not sure if people would really choose death over public speaking, but I think some people might find waterboarding to be a more pleasant alternative than the dreaded public speech. So how is it that three 14-year-old girls conquered a fear that most adults will never even attempt?

Here are the steps that they took and some good lessons for the rest of us:

1. Be prepared.

Like most of us, these girls were nervous about talking in front of a large group (kids or not, facing hundreds of faces staring at you makes many people nervous). The girls planned their approach by first forcing me into a very intimidating question and answer session in which they ascertained exactly what they were walking into. They then started rehearsing and continued to practice and edit until the program began. This was done with outrageous amounts of junk food and frequent laughing fits.

2. State your fears.

They, without even a hint of shame, admitted to each other and to me that they were really nervous, scared, and anxious about the public speaking adventure. They never belittled each other for being nervous, they just accepted this as a normal state of mind when faced with a challenging situation. They didn't make up excuses as to why they were nervous, they just owned it and pushed forward.

3. Try new things with people who love and support you.

The three of them threw out supportive and caring words throughout the whole process, "great job", "that's a good idea", "I like your shirt" etc. The one gal that has always been on the shy side stood proudly between her two friends during the presentation and when the first question was shot their way, she said with complete confidence, "I've got this one" and proceeded to belt out an answer that most adults couldn't do even after they had rehearsed. Later she was wildly praised by her two friends and she glowed from having both tackled the challenge and the support of her friends.

I know that all three girls walked away from this experience feeling more confident and accomplished. These being skills that they will need when they face a world that tells girls that they should be sexy and skinny but not necessarily strong and smart. Despite being nervous, they did it anyway and took the risk of failing, being laughed at, or criticized.

Many of the adults that I know would rather use vices or lame excuses instead of trying something scary and risking failure, myself periodically included in that list.

I learned a lot that day too. I learned that by telling them that I trusted them and showing them that trust by allowing them to do their thing, they also believed in themselves. It wasn't easy for me to step back, but I saw how much they wanted to own the experience from start to finish so I took a leap of faith with them and it was so worth the risk for all of us.

I also learned that despite the bad press about mean girls and girls not being able to work together, in this case at least, that was completely untrue. I learned that young women want to be challenged and to have different life experiences, even scary ones. Experiences that don't have a thing to do with how they look, boys, weight loss, or not getting along with other girls.

I've watched these three girls growing up and I know that they've already approached and conquered so many fears, some big and some small. I think that our world might be hard for them with outrageous media images and ideals that are harmful for young women. Yet with a lump in my throat, I watched these three fairly typical teen-aged girls do something that wasn't so typical at all and I felt joy and hope for a brilliant future for all of our daughters.

CHAPTER 39

"Not My Time" Syndrome

It is your time! Now!

When I was training to be a life coach, I was required to practice interviewing individuals. Instead of bothering strangers on the street, I instead bothered the people that I bother most, my friends. In every single practice interview, I heard some version of the statement, "It's just not my time right now." WHAT???

It appears that a lot of women out there are suffering from the debilitating NOT MY TIME SYNDROME. When might I ask is your time? How long is your life? Do you know for a fact that you will still be here tomorrow? What are you waiting for, arthritis, dementia, bad backs, wrinkles, and constant talk about your health problems until it's your time?

Sisters, life is short, act now or regret it. What is it that makes you want to fly out of bed in the morning and take on the day? Don't even think of telling me that its packing lunches, laundry, running errands, or another horrid PTO meeting! I won't believe you.

I'm not at all suggesting that these things can be avoided or aren't satisfying in some way, but I'm wondering when was the last time you felt that wonderful feeling of accomplishment, commitment, and pure passion to something that you cared about greatly?

First, ask yourself these questions:

When I was young, what did I want to be when I grew up?

If I didn't have to worry about caring for kids, a home, a spouse, what would I do with my time?

What am I planning to do when it is "my time"?

Does my day often feel excessively busy but ultimately empty as well?

Am I starting to believe that the "Housewives of" (fill in any of the shows) are decent human beings?

Next, ask yourself if there is any way you can incorporate some of your passions into your current life. Can you find an hour a day to do something just for you? (Botox doesn't count.)

How are you using the responsibilities of family as an excuse to not do something that is entirely meaningful to just you? How much more energy will you have in the day if you were doing a number of things that were important to you?

Watch your own responses and reactions. How many excuses can you come up with to not prioritize your own well being? Do they sound like this: "my kids just can't get through the day without me", "if I let my husband help out, he'll mess things up", "good mothers devote all of their attention to their families at all times", or the most depressing of all, "I'm just too tired to fit any more into my day!"

If any of these responses or excuses sounds familiar, you too are suffering from NOT MY TIME SYNDROME! The good news is that it's not too late to save yourself.

Here's what I know: your kids don't need you focusing all of your attention on them at all times and they don't need you to be a martyr. What they really need is a mom who is happy, strong, fulfilled, energetic, and able to prioritize herself as well as her family. Give yourself and your family the gift of a really well lived life by you RIGHT NOW!

Go take that cooking class, or write your book, or get a part time job, or volunteer at a woman's shelter, or work at Starbucks where everybody is happy.

Your time is right this minute and there isn't a minute to spare. NOT MY TIME SYNDROME has followed some women all the way to the grave. Don't let that be you.

CHAPTER 40

Milestones—Miserable or Magical?

I'm a bit of a romantic when it comes to life's milestones. I picture the big days as a blur of smiles, laughs, family unity, and of course, perfect weather.

On my wedding day it rained, snowed, and had a drop of sunshine, all while family members were licking wounds from an exhausting engagement period in which none of us really got along. The day itself was fine, but in no way duplicated the wedding milestone in my imagination.

My oldest son recently graduated from college. I envisioned a smiling graduate waving at his parents, proud parents snapping pictures, and equally enamored siblings sitting at the ceremony cheering their brother on. It turned out that our graduate was exhausted from a week of graduation celebrations and was slightly less than chipper throughout the weekend. Instead of sitting outside on a gorgeous campus, we were instead shuttled into a rather stuffy gym due to pending thunderstorms. Did I mention that allergy season was in full bloom and half of us were heavily dosed with allergy medicine as histamines coursed through our bodies?

After an hour into the ceremony, the graduate's siblings were hungry and shuffled off to eat. This after a solid half hour of whining because they were hungry, tired, and bored. Our graduate wasn't very motivated to take beautiful family pictures after the ceremony, so we quickly snapped a few and proceeded to the final stages of moving him out of his apartment. Did I mention the thunderstorm that hit as we were moving him out?

Feeling more than a bit let down, I was ready to call graduation weekend a mild disappointment. I started thinking of the next big milestone and how I was sure that one would be perfect.

As our two-car caravan headed out of rural Ohio, my son joined me in one car and our two youngest children went in the other car with my husband. My son and I talked for most of the seven-hour drive. We talked about his college experience, his hopes for the future, and how quickly time had passed for both of us. Those seven hours were some of the best hours of my life.

Halfway home, both cars met up at a fast food restaurant where we all laughed at some of the crazier events of the weekend. At one point, we were all laughing so hard that we were crying and all my milestone angst slipped away. The milestone magic had nothing to do with a graduation ceremony or family pictures, but rather those small but profound moments of joy that we find with those that we love the most.

No doubt I will set up silly expectations for the next family milestone, but I hope I'm wise enough to remember milestones gone by that were completely different than my expectations. I hope I can remind myself that it isn't the milestone, it's the moment. And if I keep my eyes open, I will find the magic in the milestone . . . even if there is a bit of misery along the way.

That, my sisters, is life.

Know that life is a journey with milestone after milestone. You can implement the lessons I have set out here and you can experience all the magic that your life has to offer.

You are destined to be a happy and confident woman who leads an inspired life! Take the first step now! I am cheering you on!

Thank you for reading for this book, another milestone in the journey of my life, and yes, it has been pretty magical.

If you are ready to make some big changes in your life so that you can be at peak levels of happiness and confidence, email me at Lisa@smartwomeninspiredlives.com or call me at 847-757-4021.

Here's my website for more information:
www.smartwomeninspiredlives.com

About the Author

Lisa Kaplin is a psychologist and life coach at Smart Women Inspired Lives. A nationally known speaker, she has spoken at companies such as American Management Association, Kraft, Allstate, State Farm, JPMorgan Chase, and many more. Lisa is a popular blogger and has been featured on Yahoo, MSN, Lifetime Moms, Huffington Post, Mind Body Green and many others.

Lisa lives with her husband, Ken, of 25 years and has three children, Steven, Michelle, and David. She is a life long Chicagoan and dog lover.